Preserving Your Wealth

A Guide to Colorado Probate & Estate Planning

By L. William Schmidt, Jr.

Bradford Publishing Company

Denver, Colorado

PLEASE READ

This book, *Preserving Your Wealth: A Guide to Colorado Probate & Estate Planning,* is intended to provide general information with regard to the subject matter covered. It is not meant to provide legal opinions or offer advice, nor to serve as a substitute for advice by licensed, legal professionals. This book is sold with the understanding that Bradford Publishing Company and the author, by virtue of its publication, are not engaged in rendering legal or other professional services.

Bradford Publishing Company and the author do not warrant that the information herein is complete or accurate, and do not assume and hereby disclaim any liability to any person for any loss or damage caused by errors, inaccuracies or omissions, or usage of this book.

Laws, and interpretations of those laws, change frequently and the subject matter of this book contains important legal consequences. It is the responsibility of the user of this book to know if the information contained in it is applicable to his situation, and if necessary, to consult legal, tax, or other counsel.

Library of Congress Cataloging-in-Publication Data

Schmidt, L. William.
  Preserving your wealth : a guide to Colorado probate & estate planning / by L. William Schmidt, Jr.
      p. cm.
Includes bibliographical references and index.
  ISBN 1-883726-90-5 (alk. paper)
  1. Probate law and practice—Colorado. 2. Inheritance and transfer tax—Law and legislation—Colorado. 3. Estate planning—Colorado. I. Title.

  KFC1944.S36 2003
  346.78805'2—dc21

                                        2003003828

ISBN: 1-883726-90-5
Published by Bradford Publishing Company
1743 Wazee Street, Denver, Colorado 80202

CONTENTS

Contents

PREFACE

Teachers are those who use themselves as
bridges, over which they invite their students
to cross; then having facilitated their
crossing, joyfully collapse, encouraging
them to create bridges of their own.

— Nikos Kazantzakis

The law of estate planning and probate — the law dealing with transfer of wealth during lifetime and at death — is centuries old, yet little understood. Every adult citizen should understand the purpose of probate and the people it protects, and with this understanding be motivated to plan his estate.

Every effort has been made to interpret in this book, fully and fairly, major facets of estate planning and probate — to present the subject in a well-balanced and readable form. This book is not intended to be a "do-it-yourself" substitute for carefully made estate plans prepared with the assistance of knowledgeable advisors. On the contrary, it is intended to point out the pitfalls of homemade wills and amateur decisions regarding probate and tax planning. General principles have been stated to provide an overall view of the subject. The experienced reader will notice that certain exceptions to general rules have been omitted. The author felt that the reader should have an understanding of general principles, unencumbered by exceptions. Thus, the importance of personal consultation with tax advisors proficient in the fields of estate planning and probate cannot be overemphasized.

The author had the good fortune to start his law career with the exceptional firm of Holland & Hart in Denver. His estate planning mentor and critic was the esteemed attorney, William P. Cantwell. His methods were often harsh, but his meticulous attention to detail and his invocation of the humanity required to professionally attend to the personal estate planning needs of a client have served the author well. When one looks back at those who have made an important impact on their professional life, few would have a finer example than William P. Cantwell.

DEDICATION

This book is dedicated to my mother, Violet K. Schmidt, and in loving memory of my father, Lail W. Schmidt, who taught me the importance of hard work and dedication to family. To my beloved wife and friend, Marilyn S. Schmidt, who is my encourager and gives joy to my life. To our children, Kimberly, Andrea, Darrell, and Crystal, who are our investments in the future and the objects of the planning strategies contained in this book.

ACKNOWLEDGMENTS

The author and publisher would like to thank Allen Sparkman for his enlightening chapter on Asset Protection, and Joseph A. Dawson and Marco D. Chayet for contributing a practical and informative chapter on Long-Term Care and Medicaid Planning.

We would also like to express our gratitude to Dennis N. Whitmer, Vice President and Trust Officer for Colorado State Bank and Trust in Denver, for sharing his wisdom and experience as the peer reviewer. We also appreciate the meticulous review that Julia Griffith McVey and Karen K. Hoiland, associates with Schmidt & Horen, gave various portions of the book. Finally, we wish to thank our exceptional legal reviewer, Merry H. Balson, of the Denver law firm Millard & Hunter, P.C., for her editing finesse and outstanding legal evaluation.

WHAT IS PROBATE?

*We're drowning in information and starving for
knowledge.*
— Rutherford D. Rogers

Lawyers tend to use words and phrases that have come to be
common knowledge in the profession but which have no meaning to
the average lay person. Probate is such a word. It is confusing
because it does not describe an event, but rather a process. And the
process can be complicated and frustrating if not properly anticipated and planned for. Therefore, let us begin by examining what
this mysterious process entails.

The Word "Probate"

The word "probate" originally meant "to test and to prove." It
came to mean the procedure of establishing before a court of proper
jurisdiction that an instrument is the last will and testament of a
deceased person.

In Colorado, probate has come to include not only the
determination by the probate court that an instrument is the last will
and testament of the decedent, but also the fulfillment of all those
things the appropriate probate court may do to settle estates.

Probate proceedings involve determining whether the decedent left a valid will; appointing and qualifying a personal representative for the estate; collecting the assets of the estate; preparing an inventory of the estate; preparing accountings to the beneficiaries; preparing estate, inheritance, and income tax returns; verifying and paying debts, valid claims, and taxes; selling property to pay estate liabilities or to effect estate distribution; determining those who are entitled to receive the property of the estate and distributing estate assets to the proper beneficiaries; settling the accounts of the personal representative; discharging the personal representative and releasing the sureties on any bond; and, closing the estate.

Under the Colorado Probate Code, the probate court is a separate division of the district court established in each county. The only exception is in the City and County of Denver where a separate court, called the Denver Probate Court, is assigned to handle only probate matters.

What Is a Personal Representative?

The personal representative of an estate is the person appointed by the court to act for the estate. In some states, the personal representative is called an "executor" or an "administrator." The personal representative qualifies to serve by signing an acceptance of appointment and by providing a surety bond, if a bond is required. Banks and corporations with trust powers, as well as individuals, may act in this capacity. The court will appoint as personal representative the person named in the will, unless some unusual reason compels a different appointment. A personal representative appointed in Colorado is not required to provide a bond unless the decedent has directed otherwise in the will, or unless the court determines that for some reason the bond is necessary to protect the estate.

The clerk of the court issues "letters" to a personal representative after he is appointed by the court, has filed an acceptance of appointment, and has made any bond that may be required and approved by the court. "Letters" are a printed form certified by the court clerk stating that the holder, the personal representative, is in charge of the estate and entitled to possession of the assets. "Letters" are evidence of authority to take charge of an estate and to act for it.

What Is the Estate?

The estate of a person includes everything he owns. In this sense, your estate is the aggregate of all your assets, riches, and fortune, and includes rights to receive income from property owned by another. One of the common uses of the word is to denote and describe, in a most general manner, the property and assets of a deceased person.

The probate estate of a deceased person is that part of the decedent's estate administered by the personal representative and subject to the applicable laws, terms of the will, and control of the court. It does not include property or assets of the decedent which do not pass into the hands of the personal representative, such as bank or brokerage accounts with a "POD" or "payable on death" beneficiary designation, assets titled in joint tenancy passing to a surviving joint tenant, or life insurance proceeds payable to someone other than the estate. The probate estate remains open from the date of death until all debts and taxes are paid, the property is distributed to the heirs or beneficiaries, and the court discharges the personal representative.

The probate estate should not be confused with the "taxable estate," which is defined under the federal tax laws for purposes of assessing the federal estate tax (the so-called "death tax"). A decedent may have owned or controlled property, or enjoyed income from property during lifetime that is a part of the gross estate for tax purposes, but is not a part of the probate estate. For example, the decedent may have disposed of certain assets during lifetime that continue to be a part of the gross estate for tax purposes, but not part of the probate estate. Common examples are:

1. Gifts of life insurance policies made before the death of the donor. (However, most outright gifts to any one person in any one year of a total value of $11,000 or less, adjusted in the

3

future to reflect inflation, will not be a part of the taxable estate.)

2. Conveyances of property in which the grantor reserved income or control for life.

3. Trusts created by a decedent who reserved the right to revoke, alter, or amend the trust; to control the beneficial enjoyment of the property; or, to continue to receive the income during lifetime.

What Is Not Included in the Probate Estate?

The probate estate does not necessarily include all of the property and assets owned by or for the benefit of a decedent during his lifetime. Even a person of modest means usually owns property said to be a part of the estate, but which does not pass under the person's will and never becomes a part of the probate estate. Such property may include insurance, employee benefits, social security, property held in joint tenancy, and trust property.

Life Insurance

Life insurance is payable on a person's death (the insured) to the named beneficiary in the manner provided by the policy. The death benefit is usually made payable to a named beneficiary. If the beneficiary dies prior to or simultaneously with the insured, the death benefit is made payable to a contingent beneficiary. The insured is usually the owner of the policy. The proceeds of such a policy are not payable to the personal representative of the estate of the insured and do not become a part of the probate estate. However, the proceeds will be a part of the insured's probate estate if they are made payable to the estate by the terms of the policy, or if all named beneficiaries die before the proceeds become payable. The proceeds are a part of the person's taxable estate for estate tax purposes if the insured had an "incident of ownership" in the policy, or if it was payable to the insured's estate. Incidents of ownership include such matters as the right to change the beneficiary, the right to cancel the policy, the right to take loans against the policy, and similar rights.

Annuities and Retirement Benefits

An annuity may be payable under what is known as an "annuity contract" or under an insurance policy with provisions for payment of benefits during the insured's lifetime and, perhaps, thereafter to a named successor beneficiary. An individual may be the beneficiary of an annuity created by a contract purchased by that individual or purchased by another. The individual may be an employee of a corporation that has a pension plan or profit-sharing plan under which that individual and their spouse or dependents are entitled to payments. The person's employer may have created an Individual Retirement Account (IRA), a Keogh Plan, or other form of qualified retirement plan. Any amounts payable after the death of the beneficiary will be payable according to the terms of the annuity contract, insurance policy, or pension plan. In most cases the amounts payable after the death of the beneficiary will not be a part of the probate estate.

Social Security and Government Pensions

Social Security benefits and pensions payable under federal or state law do not become part of the probate estate. These amounts may or may not be taxable. However, any amounts payable, but not actually paid, prior to the death of a beneficiary may become payable to the personal representative of the estate and become a part of the probate estate.

Bonds

United States Savings Bonds may be made payable to the decedent as owner or co-owner, or to a beneficiary named by the decedent. If the co-owner or named beneficiary survives the decedent, the survivor is the absolute owner of the bonds. In that case, the bonds do not become a part of the decedent's probate estate, although they may be included, in whole or in part, in the gross estate for estate tax purposes. Of course, these bonds will be a part of the probate estate of the surviving co-owner or named beneficiary if such person still owns them at the time of his death, and has not reissued them either to himself and another person as a co-owner, or to another person as the new named beneficiary.

Property in Joint Tenancy

Property owned by the decedent and another in joint tenancy with right of survivorship is not a part of the probate estate of the decedent. This property is often referred to as "jointly owned property." It passes to the surviving joint tenant immediately upon the death of the deceased joint owner by operation of law. No probate is required to transfer ownership. However, this assumes that a valid joint tenancy with right of survivorship has been created. To be held in joint tenancy, the title to the asset must specifically state that the owners hold title "as joint tenants with right of survivorship," "in joint tenancy," or "as joint tenants." In Colorado, there is an exception for personal property (furniture, art, household goods, etc.) owned by a husband and wife. This type of property is presumed to be owned by the spouses in joint tenancy unless a bill of sale or other writing establishes some other form of ownership.

Colorado also recognizes another form of co-ownership know as "tenancy in common." Property titled in this manner is equally owned by the parties named on the title, but there is no survivorship feature. Therefore, upon the death of either tenant in common, that person's undivided interest in the property does not vest automatically in the surviving owner, but instead passes to the person or persons named in the deceased co-owner's will.

Trust Property

Property conveyed by an individual to a trustee, to be administered in trust and distributed after the individual's death, usually is not a part of the probate estate. A person may convey property to a trustee to be held and administered in trust, with the income and property of the trust estate to be used and distributed as provided in the instrument. The person creating the trust is referred to as the settlor, the trustor, the grantor, or the trust maker. The settlor may name himself as the trustee; may reserve the right to alter, and amend, or revoke the trust during lifetime; and may make himself the beneficiary of the trust. The property of a trust of this kind generally would not be subject to administration by the personal representative of the probate estate unless the trust terminated, was revoked by the settlor prior to death, or the trust directed that the trust assets be distributed to the settlor's estate upon the death of the settlor.

If a decedent is the trustee or beneficiary of a trust created by some other person, or is entitled to receive income from, or use of property, these rights terminate upon death. The property in which these rights exist will not be part of the probate estate, except income payable to the beneficiary, or possibly other vested rights the beneficiary had in the property at the time of death. For more on the revocable living trust, see Chapter 17.

Small Estate Transfers

Since probate administration under court supervision is only necessary to transfer title to property held in the sole name of a decedent, it is possible, through the various forms of property ownership already discussed, to eliminate the need for probate. However, even though the majority of the estate assets may have been held in a form to avoid probate, there may be some property still titled, in whole or in part, in the name of the deceased owner. Colorado law provides for the transfer of a certain amount of property titled in the decedent's name without the necessity of court procedures. Where the total value of all property, less liens and encumbrances, does not exceed $50,000, such property may be transferred to the beneficiary legally entitled to it by simply executing a written affidavit in the form prescribed by statute. This procedure may not be used to transfer title to real estate. This technique can be extremely useful, but it is not a substitute for careful planning where the total elimination of probate is a major consideration.

The Probate Process

The probate process has traditionally been a very complicated, time-consuming, and costly process that has also been neither understood, nor appreciated, by the general public. It has been a breeding ground of much mischief. In 1974, Colorado adopted the Uniform Probate Code, which was a new system of probate designed to introduce choices in the probate process so that probate could be greatly simplified in the majority of cases.

The first choice involves the manner in which the decedent's last will and testament is probated. If there is no contest regarding the validity of the will or any of its provisions, it is possible to have the will informally probated without the need for testimony by the witnesses to the will, and without the need for an official court determination of the validity of the will.

If, for some reason, any person interested in the estate of the decedent requests a formal determination regarding the validity of the will, notices are sent to all interested parties and a court hearing is held to examine the will and obtain an official judicial determination of its validity.

Obviously, the formal method is more costly and time-consuming, and it would presumably be used only in cases where there is an issue of validity. Issues of validity include questions as to the authenticity of the signature of the person making the will, questions regarding the mental capacity of the testator to make a valid will, and issues relating to possible physical or mental duress.

After the will has been admitted to probate, the individual or institution named in the will as the personal representative is appointed by the court to administer the estate. A formal certificate of the court appointment, called "letters," is issued as evidence of the personal representative's authority. If there is no living and qualified personal representative named in the will, or if the decedent died intestate (without a will), the court will appoint a personal representative determined by a set priority based upon relationship to the decedent. The personal representative, by exhibiting a certified copy of the letters, can protect purchasers and others with whom he deals. Thus, as soon as letters are issued, the assets of the estate are completely marketable.

There are also choices with regard to the degree of formality with which the personal representative administers the estate. A "formal administration," if requested by the beneficiaries or ordered by the court for the protection of the estate, involves most of the complexity and delay that existed under the law before the enactment of the Colorado Probate Code. All important actions on the part of the personal representative must be approved in advance by the court. An inventory of the assets of the estate, and periodic accountings of the actions of the personal representative will ordinarily be required to be filed with the court. Formal probate would ordinarily not be desirable, except in cases where there is a great deal of distrust or hostility among beneficiaries, or between the beneficiaries and the personal representative.

Most probate proceedings in Colorado are under the "informal administration" alternative. Under this method of operation, the personal representative is authorized to possess and deal with the assets of a decedent, or to distribute the assets to the persons who are entitled to them. Notice to creditors is published in a local newspaper, giving the decedent's creditors an opportunity to file claims in the estate for payment of debts. The personal representative reviews the claims and pays those that he feels are legitimate. Claims that are disallowed by the personal representative may be submitted to the court for determination. The personal representative is entitled to continue the business of the decedent, and to act in a prudent manner to manage and deal with the estate assets. An inventory and accountings should be maintained for the information of estate beneficiaries, but these documents are not required to be filed with the court.

After all claims, including taxes, that may be due as a result of the decedent's death, have been paid or provided for, the personal representative has the responsibility of distributing the remaining assets to the beneficiaries named in the decedent's will, and if there was no will, then to the decedent's statutory heirs.

Although the administrative process may have initially been commenced informally, any person interested in the estate may, at any time, petition the court to force a formal administration with all of the notice and hearings which result.

There are even options regarding the eventual closing of the estate. This may be done informally by the personal representative filing with the court a sworn statement indicating that he has published the required notice to creditors, that all expenses of administration and claims have been paid, that the estate has been distributed to the persons entitled to the assets, and that a copy of the sworn statement has been sent to persons having an interest in the estate as a creditor or beneficiary. One of the disadvantages to this informal method of closing the estate is that the personal representative continues to be liable for all actions taken by the personal representative for one year after the filing of the closing statement.

On the other hand, the personal representative may decide to have a formal proceeding to terminate the administration of the estate by asking the court to approve a final accounting, and to approve the final distribution of the estate to the beneficiaries. This requires notice be given to all interested parties, and a hearing before the court. If the court is satisfied that everything has been properly administered, the request of the personal representative is approved and all liability terminates at that time.

The combination of choices for opening, administering, and eventually closing an estate is numerous. In a particular situation, the personal representative might decide to have a formal probate of the will, with an unsupervised or informal administration of the estate, followed by a formal closing. In most cases, however, especially where there is no conflict or disagreement among the estate beneficiaries, it is most expeditious and inexpensive to have an informal probate of the will, an unsupervised administration of the estate, and an informal closing based upon the sworn statement of the personal representative. Since the choices are so numerous, and since the consequences may be very important, it is essential to have the advice and assistance of qualified legal counsel.

Summary

Not everything a person owns or considers to be property will become a part of that person's probate estate. Large parts of the estate often go to beneficiaries outside the will. Care, then, should be taken to make certain that a sufficient amount of property (probate estate) will pass under the will to pay estate debts, take care of legacies, and accomplish the purposes intended by the will. Moreover, property may be a part of a decedent's gross estate for federal estate tax purposes, regardless of whether it is a part of the decedent's probate estate.

WHAT WILL PROBATE COST?

Of universal interest is the question, "What will probate cost my estate?" The answer involves careful consideration of the size, type, and location of the present and future assets comprising the estate income; any tax complications present; the simplicity or complexity of the disposition of the estate; the extent and type of the debts; and various other factors. This chapter will deal with costs and expenses in relatively routine administrations. It will not cover probate intricacies in unusual situations, or complicated probate litigation.

Court Costs and Bond Premiums

Court costs are set out in state law, and in schedules of charges published by the clerks responsible for handling the court papers. Such costs include an initial docket fee to cover a wide variety of court services for administration of an estate. There will be additional costs for certified copies of documents and other routine court expenses. A lawyer can make an accurate estimate of court costs once it is known whether there is a provision for an independent personal representative, whether bond has been waived, the nature and extent of the decedent's assets, whether there is a probability of litigation, and similar facts.

No bond is required of a personal representative appointed in an informal probate proceeding unless the last will and testament requires the posting of a bond, or unless a beneficiary or creditor makes a demand that bond be posted. Bond may be required by court order in a formal probate proceeding, unless the last will and testament specifically relieves the personal representative of the bonding requirement. However, any person interested in the estate may still request that a bond be posted, and the court will then determine whether it feels that protection of the estate requires the posting of a bond.

If bond is required for any reason, the amount of the bond, and its cost, will depend upon a number of factors. The purpose of the bond, of course, is to protect the estate against negligent or improper actions on the part of the personal representative resulting in damage to, or loss of, estate assets. The Colorado Probate Code contains a number of provisions that permit the court to determine the amount of the bond, and to determine whether or not security, or surety, should be provided in addition to the personal guarantee of the individual serving as personal representative.

Appraisal Fees

The personal representative may employ qualified appraisers to assist in determining the fair market value of any asset that may be subject to reasonable doubt. Different persons may be employed to appraise different kinds of assets included in the estate. The need for appraisals is especially important where there is real estate or an interest in a business. Depending upon the complexity of the property being appraised, the cost could range from a few hundred dollars, to many thousands of dollars.

Personal Representative's Fees

Under the Colorado Probate Code, the personal representative is entitled to a reasonable fee. The statute does not set the fee. This is contrary to the law as it existed before the enactment of the Code, when there was a statutory fee schedule based upon a percentage of the value of the estate.

If the will provides for a stated amount of compensation for the personal representative, but there was no lifetime contract with the decedent by the personal representative regarding compensation, the personal representative may renounce the provision in the will, and then be entitled to reasonable compensation. The personal representative may renounce his right to all or any part of the compensation by a written renunciation filed with the court. For the personal representative to avoid possible income and gift tax liability in connection with the waiver of compensation, there must be a clear and irrevocable renunciation of the right to receive the compensation.

Attorney Fees

The personal representative is entitled to employ attorneys, accountants, and any other agents that may be necessary to assist in the administration of the estate. These individuals are entitled to be paid a reasonable fee for their services. Although attorney fees in Colorado were once determined by applying a percentage figure to the total value of the property subject to probate, those fee schedules are no longer in effect. The attorney's fee is now regarded as a private matter to be agreed upon between the lawyer and client in accordance with proper standards of reasonableness. If a bank or trust company is acting as the personal representative, the services performed by the attorney for the estate will be fewer than if an individual family member is serving as personal representative. This is due to the fact that the bank or trust company will have the background and experience to perform many tasks that the attorney will need to perform if an inexperienced family member is handling the estate. Any beneficiary of the estate can request the court to review the reasonableness of attorney fees; or the court can review such fees on its own initiative.

What Is a Reasonable Fee?

The Colorado Probate Code sets forth certain factors to be considered as guides in determining the reasonableness of a fee. These factors apply in determining the fee of the personal representative, the attorney for the estate, or any other agent of the estate. The Colorado Probate Code's factors closely follow the American Bar Association's published ethical rules describing the points to be considered when determining the amount of legal fees. The following factors are to be considered under the Colorado Probate Code:

1. The time and labor required, the novelty and difficulty of the questions involved, and the skill requisite to perform the service properly.
2. The likelihood, if apparent to the personal representative, that the acceptance of the particular employment will preclude the person employed from other employment.
3. The fee customarily charged in the locality for similar services.
4. The amount involved and the results obtained.
5. The time limitations imposed by the personal representative or by the circumstances.
6. The experience, reputation, and ability of the person performing the services.

No one of these considerations, in itself, is controlling. They are merely guides in ascertaining the real value of services performed on behalf of the estate.

Summary

Colorado has led the way among American jurisdictions in streamlining its probate procedures to minimize probate costs and simplify the administration of decedents' estates, by dispensing with formal court administration. With a proper will, probate court costs are minimal and there is no bonding expense. The fees of personal representatives can be estimated once the gross value, nature of the estate, and probable income and disbursements are known.

In Colorado, attorney fees for services to the personal representative are not set by law, but are the subject of private agreement. If an attorney is required to set or estimate a fee in advance, he may suggest a small percentage figure based upon the estate's gross value. If an attorney is employed on a reasonable fee basis to be determined upon completion of his services, he may charge the personal representative a fee that will be less than an arbitrary percentage figure. Such a fee must be reasonable in light of all the considerations set out in the ethics rules published by the State Bar of Colorado. The fees of attorneys serving personal representatives under court control are subject to the approval of the probate court, and the court requires the attorney to prove the reasonableness of his charge.

When a testator does not make a proper will, the cost of administering his estate will be higher than if a properly prepared will has been made by an attorney who was naturally familiar with expense-cutting provisions, meaning of legal terms, consequences of legal principles, requirements for executing wills, and the necessity for definiteness.

A person needing the services of an attorney should not hesitate to discuss the attorney's fee or any other cost of probate with him. Substantial savings of probate costs can be affected by proper planning.

WHEN IS MY ESTATE VALUED
AND WHY?

An estate may be valued on several occasions, and may be valued for several reasons. An initial reason is to obtain facts upon which to plan the most efficient and economical transfer of the estate to the persons who are to receive the property during lifetime or after the death of the owner. Planning requires that valuation should be done during the lifetime of the owner of the property. Only with such knowledge can the estate planning professional properly guide the client in making the most tax efficient decisions regarding the disposition of the assets.

Valuation for Tax Purposes

Regardless of whether an appraisal is required during the course of probate proceedings, there must be a valuation made of the estate, whether large or small, for tax purposes. This valuation is made to enable the timely payment of any taxes due, and the distribution of the estate to the beneficiaries free of any tax lien.

An estate tax return may be required to be filed within nine months after death, depending on the value of the estate. If death occurs in 2003, a return is required if the gross estate (before any allowances for debts, expenses, or other permitted deductions) is in excess of $1,000,000. The value of the estate requiring a return is increasing under current law, and this value should be consulted at the time of death.

Valuation is determined differently for a variety of assets. Real estate is generally valued to reflect the highest and best use of the property, unless special use valuation is elected (see discussion later in this chapter). Stocks are valued based on the mean between the high and low quoted selling prices on the date of death. If the stock is in a closely held business that is not traded on an exchange, an appraisal will often be based on the value of the business assets, or by capitalizing the earnings of the business, or a combination of both. A promissory note owed to the decedent will be valued on the amount of unpaid principal plus accrued interest, unless the personal representative of the estate can prove otherwise. The value of life insurance owned by the decedent on the decedent's life is the face amount of the death benefit (not the cash surrender value of the policy during the insured's lifetime). If the decedent owns only a fractional or partial interest in property (such as an undivided interest as a joint tenant, or a minority interest in a closely-held company), the value may be discounted to reflect less than complete ownership and control.

Values Six Months after Death

Using asset values as of six months after death is commonly referred to as using the "alternate valuation date." Under federal tax laws, a personal representative can elect to use the alternate valuation date. The purpose of this provision, born of the depression days of the 1930's, is to provide tax relief where there has been a decline in the values of an estate within six months after the decedent's death.

Properties acquired from a decedent generally take a new basis for income tax purposes equal to either the fair market value on the date of the decedent's death, or, if elected, the alternate valuation date. This new basis is referred to as the "stepped-up basis." However, the alternate valuation date value may be used only if the value of the estate and the estate tax due are decreased by making the election. The alternate valuation date may not be used solely to obtain a higher income tax basis for estate assets.

An important exception to the stepped-up basis rule applies when the decedent received the property by gift within the one-year period before the decedent's death. If the person who gave the property to the decedent (the donor) reacquires the property from the decedent's estate, the basis of the property in the hands of the donor or donor's spouse will be the same basis that the decedent had before the decedent's death. This is true even though the property had a higher value at the decedent's death (or on alternate valuation date) and was subject to estate tax in the decedent's estate at the higher valuation. This exception prevents a donor from obtaining a stepped-up basis in property given to a decedent within the short period prior to the decedent's death for the purpose of minimizing the donor's income taxes on a subsequent sale by the donor after reacquiring the property from the decedent's estate.

The alternate valuation date may be used only if there is a timely filing of the federal estate tax return, and the election is made to use the alternate valuation date on that return. If the alternate valuation date is elected, then all of the property in the estate must be valued as of the alternate date. In other words, you cannot pick and choose which assets to value at the lower value. However, if the alternate valuation date is used, then any property that is distributed, sold, exchanged, or otherwise disposed of within the six months after the decedent's death, is valued at the value on the date of sale, distribution, or disposition. The value of any interest which is affected by a mere lapse of time, such as the paying out of an annuity, or the expiration of a patent, is not entitled to be revalued where the revaluation reflects only the effect of the passage of time.

Special Use Valuations

The Internal Revenue Code allows special use valuations to give relief to farmers and owners of closely held businesses. If the personal representative makes a proper election, qualified real estate (which is included in decedent's gross estate and used for farming purposes or in a closely held trade or business) may be valued for estate tax purposes based on the value of its "actual use," instead of the fair market value of its "highest or best use." For example, although a farm approached by urban expansion might have a higher market value for commercial development than for continued farming, it can be valued for estate tax purposes at its value as a farm, rather than as urban development property. The original law limits the aggregate reduction in value by such election to $750,000, plus cost of living adjustments. For an estate of a decedent dying in 2002, the aggregate decrease may not exceed $820,000.

For the special use valuation election to apply, the qualifying real property must: (a) have been used by the decedent, or the decedent's family, as a farm or in a trade or business; (b) have been so used for at least five out of eight years prior to the decedent's death, disability, or retirement; (c) have had material participation by the decedent, or the decedent's family, during such years; (d) pass from the decedent to defined members of the family; (e) have a value for the real property used in the farm or business equal to at least 25% of the adjusted gross estate; and (f) have a value for the entire farm or business, including both real property and personal property used in farming or in the trade or business, equal to at least 50% of the decedent's adjusted gross estate. The valuations used for the 25% and 50% tests are values of the highest and best use, rather than the actual use. Computations of the value of the gross estate for these tests include gifts made by the decedent within three years prior to the decedent's death. The inclusion of these gifts in the gross estate prevents deathbed gifts by the decedent of other property to qualify the farm or trade or business real property for the special use valuations.

For this purpose, a farm includes, among other things, ranches, nurseries, orchards, and, subject to other special rules, woodlands. The tax law provides a formula for determining the actual value of farms using the cash rental basis of comparable land, or if none, net share rental of comparable land, and other factors. Other methods may, however, be used for determining the actual value of the real estate used in farming or in the trade or business.

The estate tax benefits realized by these special use valuations may be recaptured by a tax imposed upon the beneficiaries who receive the property if, within 10 years after the decedent's death, the qualified property is transferred away from the defined family, or the property ceases to be used (with some exceptions) for farming or other business purposes. For further discussion regarding special use valuation, see Chapter 21.

Summary

Valuation, as discussed in this chapter, whether for the purpose of planning, fixing family allowances, determining taxes due or not due, or using the alternate valuation date, is the determination of the market value of property on the proper dates, except where special use valuations are permitted. Valuations may be determined by a variety of methods, depending on the type of property involved. Valuations for tax purposes require the application of special tax rules. The decedent can achieve the goal of passing the maximum benefits to the decedent's beneficiaries by acquiring proper valuations at the proper times.

HOW WILL MY DEBTS BE PAID?

In the course of a lifetime, every person creates debts. The size and nature of these obligations vary with individual and family situations. It is not surprising that the wealthiest people usually create the biggest debts because they have the assets, collateral, and credit rating to support larger borrowing. Unfortunately, many families of average means obligate themselves beyond their abilities to pay, causing financial problems during lifetime, and most certainly after death. The biggest obligation is usually the mortgage on the home. In addition, there may be innumerable time payments for cars, appliances, and other items. In any event, these obligations may become a factor to deal with in an estate administration.

Take the case of a husband and wife with minor children. If the spouses live to retirement, the mortgage on the home will normally be paid off, along with many other items purchased on credit. But what if the husband dies unexpectedly at an earlier age? He leaves the wife to support the minor children and pay the financial obligations. Further, a source of income — the husband's earning capacity — is gone. This situation can create quite a hardship on the surviving family members. Therefore, it is the wise man that provides protection for his family in the event of his death.

Provisions in the Will

Most wills specifically provide for the estate to pay debts, taxes, and the cost of administration. Whether or not the will so provides, the personal representative is under a general duty to pay obligations of the decedent's estate. Will provisions that are unclear may cause confusion, delays, and unnecessary expense. A direction by the testator in a will that "my just debts be paid" is unwise because it may revive debts that would otherwise be unenforceable. It is more appropriate to provide for payment of "my legally enforceable debts."

The phrase "my just debts be paid" may also be interpreted as a requirement for the personal representative to pay off installment debts and long-term mortgage obligations immediately. The careful person will avoid this danger by providing that the personal representative shall not be required to pay debts prior to maturity, but may extend or renew any debt upon such terms and for such time as he deems best. Thus, the will should explicitly state the testator's intention. Does the testator wish the home to pass to the spouse or children burdened with the mortgage, or should the home be distributed after the mortgage has been paid from other assets of the estate?

Funeral Expenses

Occasionally a testator will include detailed funeral arrangements in his will. If the testator feels strongly about some special funeral arrangements, he should communicate his feelings to some member of the family, because the will is often not readily accessible at the time of death.

Funeral expenses and items incident thereto, such as tombstones, grave markers, crypts, or burial plots, are chargeable against the estate of the decedent. As a matter of public policy, these expenses are granted a high priority for payment. If the testator does not have burial insurance, and if he has not otherwise provided for their payment in his will, then funeral expenses will be paid out of available estate assets. If prior arrangements have not been made, emotional factors at the time of death can cause excessive funeral expenses.

Estate and Inheritance Taxes

Just as funeral expenses are a kind of involuntary debt against the estate, so are taxes due because of death. The federal and Colorado estate taxes may well be, and in many instances are, the largest costs chargeable to the estate. The reader should carefully review Chapters 6 and 8 for a detailed explanation of this subject.

It is the obligation of the personal representative to pay such taxes as are due. Here again, the testator may have made other provisions to satisfy death taxes. If no provisions were made for payment, then the personal representative must look first to any available cash in the estate. If there is none, or if the cash is insufficient, then the personal representative must sell securities or other liquid assets to provide the necessary amount. Failure to provide funds for the payment of taxes may destroy the testator's intention regarding distribution of assets to his beneficiaries.

Many people may not have much cash, but they are wealthy "on paper"— that is, they may own a farm or ranch, or other assets that are considerably enhanced in value. The father may wish to leave such assets to his wife, or children, or both. If, at his death, the size of the estate is such that several thousand dollars in taxes are due, then the only alternative may be to sell all or a portion of the assets to raise the necessary funds.

The situation may arise where the decedent left sufficient assets to pay all the death taxes and other costs, but also requested that various specific gifts be made. For example, suppose the home, personal effects, and life insurance proceeds go to the wife, the farm or ranch to the sons, and stocks and bonds to the daughters. Does the testator intend each person bear his proportionate share of death taxes, or should the assets be charged against only certain portions of the estate? If insufficient cash is available, which assets should be liquidated first? The will should be clear and explicit with respect to the intention. Normally, an insured person wants the entire face amount of the proceeds of life insurance to pass to the named beneficiaries. Thus, it is important to provide in the will that neither taxes nor debts are to be charged against any insurance policies, or the proceeds of such policies.

Planning for the Payment of Debts and Taxes

There are steps that may be taken to minimize probate costs, provide for the payment of debts, and reduce estate and inheritance taxes. A few important suggestions are listed here.

1. A current trust or will, expertly drafted, may clarify many of the problems and, in addition, effect substantial tax savings.
2. A buy-sell agreement for the sale of a business interest at death that is funded with life insurance is usually ideal where the testator is a member of a partnership or a closely held business.
3. A mortgage cancellation policy on the home assures the home will remain intact.
4. Sufficient life insurance to pay all or some debts, cost of probate, and taxes, offsets such costs.
5. Investment in liquid assets that are readily marketable, such as stocks, bonds, and savings, can provide necessary immediate cash.
6. Endowment insurance on the children, designed to mature at the time they are ready for college, will insure future security.
7. Gifts to children or grandchildren, directly or through trusts, give assets to those the testator ultimately wants to provide for. Gifts may also affect substantial tax savings.
8. A consistent program of saving also insures future security.
9. Careful selection of a personal representative with knowledge, skill, permanency, and financial responsibility, is necessary because of the complicated nature of many estates. Selection of an appropriate personal representative

may dictate the use of professional help from a bank trust department.

10. Contracting during lifetime for only those obligations that can be paid without financial strain minimizes after-death indebtedness.

11. Consideration of educational, religious, or other charitable institutions as the ultimate beneficiary of the estate is particularly appropriate for a family without children. Even though the surviving spouse may have the benefit of the estate for life, tax savings may be substantial if title rests ultimately in a charity, since gifts to charity are generally tax-free.

Before embarking on any or a combination of these suggestions as part of a formal estate plan, the advice of competent counsel should be sought.

Summary

An unchangeable fact of our existence seems to be death, debts, and taxes. How debts and taxes are paid after death varies in direct proportion to the thought and planning given to them before death. A person who does not avail himself of the wealth of professional estate-planning talent available today is indeed unwise.

There is no substitute for competent legal advice. Home drawn or do-it-yourself wills usually cause endless litigation, and can penalize the family by higher costs and increased taxes. One improper sentence in a will may cause the estate to be improperly taxed, and thus destroy the great advantages that are legally available.

The fee for an attorney to prepare a trust or will which makes proper provision for payment of the debts is small compared to the savings affected and the avoidance of costly delays in probate administration.

TIME SCHEDULE FOR
ESTATE ADMINISTRATION

The time necessary to have a will probated, or to have an estate administered by the probate court if there is no will, is often given as a argument against permitting an estate to go through probate. Actually, Colorado probate procedure is time consuming only if the particular circumstances warrant it. A poorly planned or drawn will may require extended probate because of disagreements among the beneficiaries of the estate. An ambiguous will may require time to construe and interpret. Certain real property title transfers, and the handling of certain business interests at death, simply cannot be disposed of overnight.

Duties of the Personal Representative

What is involved in Colorado probate and administration? In Colorado, a personal representative (also referred to as an executor or administrator in other states) operates under a simplified procedure, and has important duties, some of which must be performed whether or not a living trust has been used by the decedent.

When a Colorado resident dies, the personal representative named in the will sees that burial instructions in the will, or in a letter to the personal representative or funeral home, are properly carried out even before the will is probated. Unprotected assets such as securities, cash, jewelry, and perishable assets must be secured. The personal representative determines whether there is adequate insurance against loss. The personal representative confers with the heirs, finds out whether the surviving spouse has sufficient funds to meet current living expenses, whether there is a bank or savings account to which the survivor can have interim access, and whether any other problems need immediate attention. The personal representative helps with the proof of death for insurance purposes, and generally prepares to collect the assets of the estate, which will be the personal representative's responsibility when the will is probated.

Next, the personal representative must locate the will, and have an attorney file it for probate. After being appointed by the court, the personal representative now begins the task of finding out what the estate consists of. The personal representative must locate all bank and savings accounts, and transfer them to a proper account in the name of the estate. The personal representative must identify and determine the terms of all certificates of deposit. The personal representative obtains custody of securities, which may or may not be transferred into the personal representative's name as personal representative, depending on how long the estate will be in administration. The personal representative must assume authority over any business owned by the estate, and make arrangements for its management, protection, and continuance so that, if possible, no loss of value or personnel will occur. The personal representative must locate and take possession of all other assets of the estate. The personal representative must keep detailed records of all the personal representative's actions to be sure everything is done properly.

The personal representative must not let estate property get mixed with the personal representative's own property, or with the property of any other person. There may be problems with assets that are scattered in different states, or even in foreign countries. The personal representative must collect all the money owed the estate.

The personal representative has the power to compromise, abandon, or sue for collection of any claim that the estate has, and must take appropriate and timely action on all claims.

A detailed inventory of estate assets should be made, and either filed with the court or sent to the beneficiaries of the estate. Any interested person can, of course, ask the court to appoint appraisers. The personal representative must estimate how much cash is needed to pay funeral bills, medical bills, current bills, and other debts, as well as taxes and administration expenses. The personal representative must set aside estate assets for any specific cash legacies in the will. If it is necessary to liquidate any assets to provide funds for payment of debts and cash gifts, then the personal representative must see this is done. The personal representative must determine the advisability of sale, as opposed to retention of assets for future family use, and then arrange and conduct any necessary sales.

The personal representative must properly estimate, provide for, and pay the income taxes that will be due for the portion of the year that had elapsed prior to the decedent's death. The personal representative must also take care of the estate's income taxes because the estate is a separate income taxpayer. Additionally, the personal representative must plan for and pay any Colorado and federal estate taxes using estate assets.

The personal representative must collect income as it comes in, and should watch investments so that appropriate action can be taken to protect estate values. If, for example, the price of a stock held by the estate is going down, perhaps it should be sold in favor of a more promising investment.

At the end of the period of administration, the personal representative must distribute the estate in accordance with the will. The personal representative must determine the timing of distributions to beneficiaries with a view toward the most advantageous income tax effect. Here, the personal representative must take account of, and reconcile, as far as reasonably possible, any conflicts of interest that arise among the several beneficiaries. If the will calls for the setting up of trusts, the personal representative must determine when, and to what extent, trusts are to be set up, as well as determining which assets should be used to fund the trusts. Handling this properly can mean important tax savings.

The period of the personal representative's administration is over after distribution of the estate has been effected, and all other disbursements have been properly made.

Time Sequence of Administration

Proving the Will

With this brief outline of the personal representative's duties, one may more easily understand a timetable of the events of probate. In the typical case, the family makes an effort to locate the will immediately after death in case it contains specific instructions dealing with burial. On rare occasions, the will contains bequests of organs of the body, although a Colorado driver's license notation is much more likely to be effective for that purpose. If there are such instructions, they must be carried out at once. The will is then lodged with the appropriate court.

The total elapsed time to this point may be three or four weeks, depending on how quickly the initial information is assembled. Because most wills are self-proved in Colorado, there is no necessity, even in formal probate proceedings, for the time-consuming process of searching for the witnesses to the will to prove its proper execution. Self-proof provides this necessary element of proving proper execution, provided no contention is raised at the time of probate that the testator was incompetent or unduly influenced when the will was made.

Collecting and Valuing Property

Immediately after appointment by the court, the personal representative begins the process of collecting and identifying the assets and determining their respective values. Time involved here depends on the nature and complexity of the estate, and the availability and completeness of accounting and other property records. If there are few assets and no claims of consequence, the process of identifying the assets is simple. Valuation for tax purposes may or may not consume an appreciable amount of time, depending on the kind and quantity of the assets involved, and whether an appraisal is necessary. If the assets are personal property (household furniture, jewelry, and the like), the period of valuation is relatively short. Essentially, the time element depends on how soon the appraisers can fit an appraisal into their schedules. Usually, only a week or two is involved in this process. Real estate appraisals, on the other hand, generally take longer, partly because the number of persons qualified and available to do real estate appraisals is relatively small, and it takes longer for one of these appraisers to find time to examine the property and make the actual appraisal. The more numerous or sizeable or unique the pieces of real estate, the more time is required for fair and reasonable evaluation.

Understanding the process of real estate appraisal also aids understanding the time requirements. Properties which are similar in type and use to the property owned by the estate will have generally the same characteristics, so the appraiser may arrive at the value of a property by considering recent sales of other, comparable properties in the area. Sound evaluation requires that such real estate information be assembled, sorted, and assessed. Although no sale of the estate property is contemplated, it is necessary to establish the fair market value of that property. One must answer a hypothetical question: "What would a buyer have been willing to pay a seller who was willing to sell on the date of the decedent's death?" While the answer is a matter of opinion, it should have some rational basis that can be documented and made part of the appraisal.

Another kind of property that requires time to value is stock in a closely held corporation. Valuation of listed stock is simple since immediately available market quotations show comparable sales. In contrast, a family corporation in which there may not have been a sale for many years, and in which sales that have occurred may not be representative because of special surrounding circumstances, presents a much more complex problem. A sole proprietorship presents similar problems in locating and identifying sales of similar businesses. Every closely held business is unique, and this uniqueness must be sought out and then, if necessary, demonstrated to the taxing authorities. In all these cases, valuation takes time.

A testator's careful preparation for this valuation process can save a personal representative a great deal of time. If the testator leaves a detailed list of assets, accompanied by much of the necessary data for appraisal purposes, as well as data showing original cost, and the cost of subsequent improvements, the personal representative's job is simplified and shortened.

Paying Creditor Claims

A personal representative moves at his own speed after he has prepared an inventory of the estate. He may take a reasonable time to pay claims against the estate. If the claims are few and uncomplicated, payment of those claims can be made rapidly, and the estate readied for distribution to the beneficiaries. If litigation arises, or if claims are disputed, the personal representative has adequate opportunity to dispose of these matters in the sensible, normal way that the testator could have done had he lived.

The personal representative may choose to publish a notice to creditors. This must be done in a paper of general circulation in the county of probate. If the decision is made to publish, notice is published once a week for three consecutive weeks. All claims must be presented within four months of the date of first publication, or they are forever barred. If a claim is presented, the personal representative can either pay it or disallow it. Since the personal representative has 60 days from the end of the creditor's period to deny the claim, it is a good idea to wait for the end of the claim period to review all claims. Any claim disallowed by the personal representative is permanently barred, unless the creditor commences a petition for a hearing on the claim, or an action against the personal representative within 60 days after the disallowance. If the personal representative does not act on the claim within the permitted period, the claim will be deemed allowed. Consultation with counsel during this period is very critical. If the personal representative decides that no notice is to be published, claims can be filed within one year of the death. In either instance (publication or not), Colorado law prescribes a priority for claims that must be complied with in order to avoid personal liability of the personal representative; again, an attorney should be consulted.

Accounting and Distribution

As soon as taxes and debts have been paid, the personal representative is ready to make distribution to the beneficiaries under the terms of the will, or under the intestacy laws. If the administration is not court-supervised (formal probate) and no formal closing is desired, the personal representative has no duty to make any final accounting, unless his actions are challenged by a beneficiary. It is wise to prepare a distribution statement for the information of the beneficiaries, and proceed to make distributions based upon that statement. Depending on the nature of the assets, the identity and financial circumstances of the beneficiaries, and any resulting conflicts of interest among them, the personal representative will work to reconcile differences and make the most beneficial asset distribution.

Once the asset allocation is determined, actually preparing the distribution statement and making the necessary distribution is essentially a paperwork chore. Where there is no conflict among the beneficiaries, and all are aware of the respective interests, such a distribution list may be unnecessary. If adequate accounting records are maintained, they may suffice. However, if a formal closing is used, the personal representative must prepare a formal final account to be filed with the court. Notice must be given to the heirs, along with an opportunity to question the account, and a court order must be obtained approving the account and directing the distribution. Once the court approves the account and the distribution schedule, the distribution itself can be made, followed by a report to the court that the distribution has been made, and an order from the court approving the report and discharging the personal representative.

Federal Estate Tax

One of the chief reasons for a lengthy probate administration is the nature of the federal tax law. The federal estate tax return must be filed within nine months after the date of the decedent's death. This extended period stems from the fact that federal tax law permits an estate to be valued either as of the date of death, or as of six months after the date of death, with the personal representative having the option of paying tax at the lower of the two values — an option first granted during the depression of the 1930's. If assets have declined in value since the date of death, it may be desirable to wait until the alternate valuation date has passed to determine if a tax saving is possible. Thus, for the protection of the estate, the appraisals mentioned previously have to be made twice — once as of the date of death and again as of six months later. Little, if any, extra time or expense of the appraisers is required for making the second valuation, since most of the work will have been done in the date-of-death appraisal.

The personal representative will usually find it wiser to postpone paying estate tax until it is due, giving the estate the benefit of the use of the money as long as possible. If the estate consists in large part of a farm or ranch, or other closely held business, installment payment of the estate tax is permitted. This allows time for assets to be sold at other than distress prices, and for funds to be accumulated from income, to avoid sales of property that should be retained for the family. Timing in these cases, although it involves delay in distribution, works to the benefit of the heirs.

Income Tax

The federal income tax may cause an even longer extension of the administration period. For federal income tax purposes, the estate — which comes into being at the moment of death — is a separate taxpayer, with a separate exemption, and a separate applicable tax bracket. During the period that the estate exists, it provides a separate pocket into which income may be placed, and on which federal income tax is payable at a bracket that may be lower than the brackets for either the decedent or the beneficiaries. If the tax bracket applicable to the beneficiaries is higher than that applicable to the estate, it will benefit the beneficiaries to maintain the estate as a taxpayer for as long as permissible under federal law.

Estates that remain open from two to five years or more are probably kept open mainly for federal tax reasons, rather than delinquency, procrastination, or mismanagement. The simple truth is that a personal representative who does his job thoroughly will not close the estate so long as it is in the best interest of the beneficiaries to keep it open, assuming that he operates within the permissible rules laid down by the Internal Revenue Service and by the courts. The testator's, and subsequently the personal representative's, planning and judgment will determine whether keeping the estate open for a substantial period is advantageous to the beneficiaries.

Summary

The time required to administer an estate depends on many factors — the size of the estate, the complexity of the assets, the difficulty in valuing the assets, the waiting period to obtain approval of the estate tax return by the I.R.S. when there is a taxable estate, potential conflicts among beneficiaries concerning the division of the assets of the estate, and the diligence of the attorney for the estate. Since the closing of an estate has no set deadline, the completion of the tasks required to complete the administration requires the personal representative and the attorney to keep focused on the many details involved in the process.

THE FEDERAL ESTATE TAX

*If you don't like what you get with taxation without representation,
wait 'til you see what you get with taxation with representation.*

— The Farmers Almanac

When first enacted in 1916, the modern federal estate tax affected only families of great wealth. From time to time since then, this tax has affected varying percentages of Americans. At the time of this writing, the federal estate tax impacts only about 1% to 2% of families. Accordingly, it is often thought of as a tax only upon the rich. However, as the values of real estate and stocks have risen (and often fallen from great heights), the federal estate tax may become one of the most formidable obstacles in passing a family farm, or other business, to a person's children. "The Economics of the Estate Tax," published by The Joint Economic Committee of the 105th Congress in 1998, concludes that gift and estate taxes are a leading cause of the dissolution of thousands of family run businesses.

In considering the purpose of having a federal death tax, it is important to know that the estate tax serves several purposes. Obviously, one important aspect of any tax is the raising of revenue for the operation of the federal government. However, various taxes also are designed to induce investment decisions, and implement social policy.

For example, the capital gains tax on the sale of appreciated assets, such as stocks and real estate, is the subject of constant Congressional debate and modification. A high capital gains tax discourages the sale of appreciated property. A lower capital gains tax encourages the sale of such assets and reinvestment of the proceeds (after the government takes its share of the profit) in new plants and equipment.

The social policy underlying the estate tax is the belief that "unreasonable" accumulation of wealth in the private sector is socially, politically, and economically undesirable. Therefore, the transfer of "excessive" wealth from one generation to the next is regulated by the estate tax. It is believed by some who favor the continuation of a tax levy on estates at death that the unregulated amassing of huge estates will eventually lead to the bulk of our national resources being owned by a few wealthy families. There is also prevalent the philosophy that each generation should earn its own wealth, and that we should not foster the spawning of a generation of "trust babies."

Those alert to the effects of the estate tax should take steps during their lifetimes to minimize its impact, and make preparation for payment of it. The federal government approves, indeed encourages, proper tax planning, and rewards with substantial savings those who act to minimize the tax. We all face income taxes annually, but estate taxes are faced only after death, at a time everyone tends to regard as too remote for present consideration. This chapter is designed to familiarize the reader with the federal estate tax, the way it will affect an estate, and how to prepare for it.

Federal Transfer Tax

To understand how the federal estate tax works, it is necessary to realize that the estate tax is part of an overall federal transfer tax system that includes both gift taxes and estate taxes. There is a single, or unified, rate of tax for all taxable transfers, whether the taxable transfer is made during lifetime or at death, and there is a unified tax credit (discussed later in this chapter) which makes a certain portion of those, otherwise taxable, transfers exempt from taxation. The unified credit creates a transfer tax exemption that can be used to avoid both gift tax on lifetime transfers, and estate tax on transfers at death. However, to the extent that the unified credit has been used to shield lifetime transfers, the amount of credit effectively available at death is reduced.

What Is the Gross Estate?

The federal estate tax is imposed on the transfer of a decedent's property to his beneficiaries. The tax is based on the fair market value of the assets of the estate at the time of the decedent's death, or, at the option of the personal representative of the estate, on the fair market value of the estate assets six months after the date of death (the "alternate valuation date"). In addition, there is a special valuation procedure for farm and certain other real property used in a trade or business which may be elected in certain limited circumstances. (See Chapter 21 for an expanded discussion.) In a community property state (Colorado is not a community property state), the decedent's estate includes the entire value of all that person's "separate" property, as well as the decedent's one-half interest in all community property. (For more on community property, see Chapter 16.)

The value of the estate for tax purposes includes many things in addition to the property owned outright by the decedent (such as real property, stocks, bonds, cash, and personal effects) at the time of death. The taxpayer should be aware that the following items might be included in the value of the estate for tax purposes:

1. *Insurance on the decedent's life in which the decedent possessed any "incident of ownership" at the time of the decedent's death.* In addition to actual ownership of the policy, an incident of ownership includes the right to change the beneficiary, the right to borrow against the policy, or other similar rights available under an insurance policy.

2. *Certain property that the decedent conveyed during lifetime.* Certain gifts made during lifetime, which are in excess of the annual gift tax exclusion amount, are included as part of the taxable estate. All gifts of life insurance made within three years of death are included as part of the taxable estate.

3. *Property transferred by the owner during life but in which there are certain rights retained.* These rights include the right to use the property or the income from the property for life, the right to revoke the transfer, the right to designate who should possess or enjoy the property at some future time, or in certain circumstances the right to vote stock which has been transferred during lifetime.

4. *Joint tenancy property.* The decedent's interest in property owned with another as joint tenants with the right of survivorship.

5. *Property over which the decedent held a power of appointment or other right to direct disposition.* If the decedent held a right to direct the disposition of property at the decedent's death, or upon some other event, the value of that property may be included in the decedent's estate for estate tax purposes. For example, if the decedent held a lifetime or testamentary general power of appointment giving him the right to direct that property be distributed to anyone, including the decedent, his estate, his creditors, or the creditors of his estate, the value of that property would be treated as owned by the decedent, and therefore, taxable in the decedent's estate.

From the foregoing it can be seen that determining what property constitutes a part of the decedent's estate and the value of that property for tax purposes can be complex.

Deductions and the Taxable Estate

After determining what assets are included in the gross estate, the Internal Revenue Code allows for the subtraction of various deductions in calculating the taxable estate. These include funeral expenses; attorney fees, court costs, appraisal fees, and other expenses in administering the decedent's estate; the marital deduction for transfers to or for the benefit of a surviving spouse (see Chapter 7); charitable gifts (see Chapter 10); and the qualified family-owned business interest deduction (see Chapter 21). After these deductions are subtracted from the value of the gross estate, you arrive at the taxable estate. It is this value that is taxed at progressive rates.

Computing the Tax

The federal estate tax is a progressive tax much like the income tax. The rate increases with the value of the estate. At one time, there were separate estate taxes and gift taxes. However, there is now a single "unified" tax which combines lifetime and death transfers for tax purposes. Every taxpayer is entitled to a cumulative tax exemption for transfers during life and at death. This exemption is referred to as the "applicable exclusion amount." The applicable exclusion amount results in the exemption from taxation of estates under a certain size. This amount is currently scheduled to increase over several years as reflected in Illustration 6-1.

The applicable exclusion amount is first applied to lifetime gifts that exceed the gift tax "annual exclusion." The annual exclusion allows tax-free gifts each year to an unlimited number of donees so long as such gifts do not exceed a specified amount per donee ($11,000 in 2002). Gifts in excess of the annual exclusion must be reported on a gift tax return, and are applied to and reduce the applicable exclusion amount. Therefore, no tax is imposed on lifetime gifts until the total amount of such gifts in excess of the annual exclusion exceed the applicable exclusion amount. If the total lifetime gifts in excess of the annual exclusions exceed the applicable exclusion amount, a gift tax would be assessed and payable as of April 15 of the year following the year the gift in excess of the annual exclusions and applicable exclusion amount was made.

At death, all taxable gifts (those in excess of the annual exclusions) are added to the remaining taxable estate owned by the decedent. If the total of such lifetime gifts and the assets remaining at death exceed the applicable exclusion amount, a tax applies to the excess amount. At death, any gift tax will be allowed as a credit against any estate tax payable. While the applicable exclusion amount under current law is set to increase over several years, it is important to note that the gift tax applicable exclusion amount after 2003 does not increase.

Sound confusing? It is. Illustration 6-1 shows the maximum tax rates and the applicable exclusion amounts which exist at the time of this writing. However, it is widely expected that the exclusions and the rate structure will be changed in the next couple of years. Therefore, it is important to check frequently with your tax advisors to determine the status of the law and how the expected changes will affect your estate plan.

Estate Tax Credits

After the tax has been calculated, this tax can be reduced by four credits. A credit is a direct "reduction" of the amount of tax payable (as distinguished from a "deduction" which serves to reduce the amount taxable). These credits include:

1. *State death taxes.* A credit is allowed against the federal estate tax for the amount of any estate, inheritance, or similar death tax paid to any state or the District of Columbia attributable to property included in the gross estate. The amount of this credit is based on a table contained in the Internal Revenue Code and is subject to various limitations.

Illustration 6-1

Transfer Tax Exemptions and Rates

Year	Tax Rate	Exemption
2001	55%	675,000
2002	50%	1,000,000
2003	49%	1,000,000
2004	48%	1,500,000
2005	47%	1,500,000
2006	46%	2,000,000
2007	45%	2,000,000
2008	45%	2,000,000
2009	45%	3,500,000
2010	Repeal	Repeal
2011	55%	1,000,000

2. *Estate taxes paid on prior transfers.* A credit is allowed against the estate tax for any federal estate tax paid on property received by a decedent from a prior decedent who died within 10 years before, or within 2 years after, the present decedent's death. It is not necessary that the transferred property be identified in the present decedent's estate, or even that the property still exist at the time of the second decedent's death. The maximum credit is allowed for 2 years after the prior decedent's death; after that, the credit is reduced by 20% every 2 years. In the third and fourth years, therefore, only 80% of the maximum credit is allowed, and this reduces to 20% in the ninth and tenth year. There is no credit after 10 years.

3. *Foreign death taxes.* A credit is allowed against the estate tax for any estate, inheritance, or similar death tax actually paid to a foreign country by the decedent's estate. Again, such credit is subject to various limitations set out in the Internal Revenue Code.

4. *Credit for Gift Tax Paid.* As mentioned above, a credit is allowed for gift tax paid during the decedent's lifetime if the transferred property is included in the decedent's estate.

Minimizing the Tax

Proper estate planning can minimize the federal estate tax. It is possible to use both the applicable exclusion amount (also referred to as "exempt amount") and the unlimited marital deduction to minimize, or possibly entirely eliminate, the estate tax. At a minimum, it is possible to defer the tax until the death of the last spouse. The planning strategy is to make certain that the exempt amounts of both spouses are utilized.

Illustration 6-2 shows the result of a simple estate plan in which everything passes to the surviving spouse. The illustration assumes a total estate valued at $1,200,000. This is only slightly above the exempt amount in effect at the time this book is being written. Assume the husband dies in 2002. Because of the unlimited marital deduction, there is no estate tax at his death. However, assuming the wife dies the following year with the value of the estate remaining the same, since the value of the estate exceeds the exempt amount, the children must pay an estate tax of $82,000. This is because the couple has utilized only one exemption — that of the surviving spouse — rather than utilizing the exemptions of both spouses which would have eliminated the tax payable by the children.

The solution to this tax problem involves the use of a trust which gives the surviving spouse the use of the entire estate, but only taxes a portion of the estate at her death. Illustration 6-3 shows how this works. The husband creates a trust that provides that his exempt amount remains in his trust for the benefit of the wife during her lifetime. The wife receives outright only that amount in excess of the husband's exemption. The combination of the marital deduction for the amount passing to the wife, together with the husband's exempt amount which was left in the trust, eliminates any tax at the husband's death.

Illustration 6-2

Tax Results Without Trust

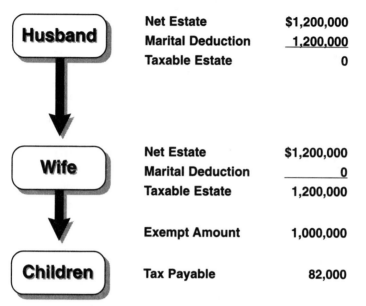

Husband	Net Estate	$1,200,000
	Marital Deduction	1,200,000
	Taxable Estate	0

Wife	Net Estate	$1,200,000
	Marital Deduction	0
	Taxable Estate	1,200,000
	Exempt Amount	1,000,000

| **Children** | Tax Payable | 82,000 |

The wife can be named as the trustee of the trust, and can be authorized to use the trust assets for her health, education, and support, and for the health, education, and support of children. Properly drafted, the remaining trust assets are not treated as owned by the wife at her death, and, therefore, pass tax-free to the children. The wife's estate then consists only of the $200,000 of assets she received outright, and her exempt amount can be used to eliminate tax on those assets.

One further observation. For this plan to work, the husband must agree to die first — a promise difficult to extract from most husbands. Otherwise, we have lost the ability to use the exemption of the wife, since she died before receiving any assets from the husband. The solution to this problem is at Illustration 6-4, and involves splitting the family assets between the spouses while both are living. The husband and wife each create a trust that provides benefits for the survivor. In this way, the order of death is immaterial (for tax

Illustration 6-3

Tax Savings With One Trust

Husband's Trust	**FIRST DEATH:**
	Net Estate $1,200,000
	Marital Deduction 200,000
	Taxable Estate 1,000,000
Wife $200,000 / **$1,000,000 Trust Continues For Support of Wife**	Exempt Amount 1,000,000
	Tax Payable 0
	SECOND DEATH:
	Net Estate $ 200,000
	Marital Deduction 0
	Taxable Estate 200,000
Children	Exempt Amount 200,000
	Tax Payable 0

purposes), since both spouses will have guaranteed the use of their respective applicable exclusion amounts. Illustration 6-4 shows the death of the husband first; however, if the wife is the first to die, simply reverse the diagram. The two trusts represent separate tax-exempt boxes that can each control up to the maximum applicable exclusion amounts.

Paying the Tax

As a general rule, the estate tax must be paid in cash nine months after the date of death. The need to pay the estate tax, coupled with other cash demands upon the estate, make it desirable to prepare a proper estimate of the tax liability and make proper provisions for payment. "Liquidity" is the term applied to provision for payment of the federal estate tax and other liabilities. Planning liquidity carefully will insure that the estate will not be forced to raise tax funds by selling assets at an unfavorable time or assets that are difficult to sell. It should be noted that the unlimited marital deduction, which

Illustration 6-4

Tax Savings With Two Trusts
(Assumes That Husband Dies First)

$1,200,000

Husband's Trust
$600,000

Wife's Trust
$600,000

TAX

Wife has Use
for Life for
Health and Support

TAX   **Children**

allows for deferral of all taxes until the death of the surviving spouse, has, to a certain extent, removed the liquidity problem in the estate of the first spouse to die.

Under certain circumstances, the personal representative of an estate may obtain an extension of time within which to pay the estate tax. For "reasonable cause," the Internal Revenue Service can allow an estate up to 10 years to pay the tax with interest (the interest rate varies in relation to the prime rate). The reasonable cause provision is frequently granted, and extension of time to pay taxes is generally allowed if a sufficient payment is made on the tax liability equal to the value of the estate's liquid assets. In addition, a 15-year install-ment payment plan is available if a specific portion of the estate con-sists of certain assets such as a closely held business. Under the 15-year payment plan, part of the estate tax bears interest at a rate of 4%. The interest rate on the balance varies in relation to the prime rate (see Chapter 21 for more on this subject).

Summary

Death and taxes are said to be inevitable. The federal government gives each person an opportunity to plan his estate in a way that minimizes the effect of the federal estate tax. Since the building of an estate is difficult, everyone should become familiar with the provisions of the federal estate tax and prepare for it.

WHAT IS THE
MARITAL DEDUCTION?

"Marital deduction" is an estate tax term that only applies to married couples, and it is a fairly complex subject. However, it can be critically important to people of moderate to substantial wealth. If the federal estate tax is eventually repealed, this discussion of the marital deduction will be meaningless since it is only an estate tax issue.

History of the Marital Deduction

The marital deduction concept is easier to grasp if you know something about its history. (The differences between "community property" and "separate property" are discussed in detail in Chapter 16.) In a community property state, any property acquired by either spouse during the marriage is considered to be owned by the two spouses equally. On the other hand, in a separate property state (also referred to as a "common law state"), assets acquired during marriage by the husband are considered to be his separate property, and property acquired by the wife is considered to be her separate property. In a community property state, even though all of the property has been acquired with the earnings of just one spouse, and even though the title to all of the property is in the sole name of that spouse, only one-half of the community property is subject to estate tax upon that spouse's death. On the other hand, in a separate property state, if all of the property is acquired from the earnings of one of the spouses, and if the title to the property is in that spouse's name, then the entire value of the property is subject to estate tax in that spouse's estate.

In 1942, Congress undertook to eliminate this tax inequality between community property and separate property states. Its approach was to provide that 100% of community property would be taxed, with certain exceptions, upon the death of the spouse in whose name the property was titled.

That approach created as many problems as it solved, so in 1948 the law was changed again and the marital deduction was born. Simply stated, that law authorized an estate tax deduction for property passing to a surviving spouse, with a limit equal to one-half the value of the decedent's separate property. Thus, in a common law state the husband could leave up to half of his property to his spouse, take the estate tax marital deduction, and achieve the same tax result as a deceased husband in a community property state. For residents of community property states, the marital deduction applied only to a spouse's separate property.

The Tax Reform Act of 1976 modified the estate tax to a "unified transfer tax system," and for the first time the marital deduction could be taken, to a limited extent, for community property passing to a surviving spouse.

Then, with enactment of the Economic Recovery Tax Act of 1981, came a sweeping change in the form of the "unlimited marital deduction." Now, one spouse may transfer any amount of property, either during life or at death, to the other spouse without tax and without regard to whether community property or separate property is being transferred. In tax language, we say that there is an unlimited marital deduction for property transferred to a spouse for gift tax purposes on lifetime transfers, and for estate tax purposes on death time transfers, emphasizing again that it no longer matters whether the transferred property is separate or community. In fact, for a lifetime gift to a spouse, a gift tax return does not have to be filed, regardless of the value of the gift. (For more on Gift Taxes see Chapter 9).

There is an important exception to the marital deduction rules that applies to transfers to a non-citizen spouse. For lifetime gifting purposes, if the spouse is not a citizen, only $100,000 each year may be gifted without gift tax consequences. This is an important exception to remember. For a lifetime gift in excess of this amount to be tax-free to a non-citizen spouse, the gift must be in the form of a special trust referred to as a QDOT, discussed in more detail below.

The Marital Deduction and the Applicable Exclusion

For estate tax planning purposes, it is easy to jump to the conclusion that everything should simply be left to the surviving spouse since the marital deduction will protect the transfer from tax. This conclusion is a case of tax planning myopia because it ignores the consequences of the subsequent transfer of the estate from the surviving spouse to the children.

As was demonstrated in Chapter 6, in larger taxable estates, it is important to maximize the applicable exclusion amount available to every person's estate by not stacking all the assets in the estate of the surviving spouse. However, since the trust of the first spouse to die can only protect that spouse's exempt amount, the portion of the estate that exceeds the exempt amount is transferred to the surviving spouse so that the combination of the marital deduction and the exempt amount will prevent any tax being due at the first death.

The next issue is the method for transferring the marital deduction amount to the surviving spouse. The most obvious method is to simply give the marital deduction amount outright to the surviving spouse. However, there are family situations where an outright distribution may be undesirable. If the surviving spouse is physically or psychologically handicapped, and would lack the capacity to effectively manage the assets in the spouse's best interests, having the assets held in a trust for the benefit of the spouse is more prudent. In the case of a second marriage, it may be desirable to give the surviving spouse the benefit of having support provided from the assets during the spouse's lifetime, while providing that the remaining assets at the spouse's death be distributed to the children or heirs of the deceased spouse, rather than to the children or heirs of the surviving spouse. If the surviving spouse has serious creditor problems, or is facing potential bankruptcy, leaving the assets in trust for the spouse can provide protection of the assets. The solution is to create a Marital Deduction Trust.

Marital Deduction Trusts

The estate tax law permits a marital deduction for transfers to a trust for the benefit of a surviving spouse, as long as the trust meets certain strict requirements. Failure of the trust to meet these requirements will result in the disqualification of the marital deduction with potentially costly estate tax consequences.

The one essential ingredient of all marital deduction trust arrangements is that the trust must be structured so that it will be taxable in the surviving spouse's estate; otherwise, a marital deduction will not be allowed in the first spouse's estate. There are four kinds of marital deduction trusts. The following analysis describes the minimum requirements for marital deduction trust qualification.

Power of Appointment Trust

One of the most common marital deduction trust formats is the "power-of-appointment trust" in which the surviving spouse (a) receives all of the income at least annually during lifetime, and (b) has the power (whether exercised or not) to either make unlimited principal withdrawals during the surviving spouse's lifetime, or to specify by will who receives the trust when the surviving spouse dies (a "power of appointment" in legal terms). The power of appointment must allow the spouse to designate any beneficiary the spouse desires. No limitation can be placed on the discretion of the spouse. The unlimited nature of the power of appointment may make this type of trust unacceptable where the spouse creating the trust wants to control the eventual beneficiaries of the property.

Estate Trust

An "estate trust" also qualifies for the marital deduction. This form of marital deduction trust differs from the power of appointment trust in that income may be accumulated in the trust, rather than having it automatically distributed to the surviving spouse each year. The trust remaining at the death of the surviving spouse, including accumulated income, must be distributed to the spouse's estate when he dies. This type of trust may be useful where the spouse is incapacitated, and distribution of the income would be unwise. It was formerly used to save income taxes, since the trust would be taxed on the accumulated income, rather than having the income taxed by a spouse who already was in a high income tax bracket. However, since income tax brackets are now compressed, this strategy is of less significance. As a result, the estate trust is rarely used.

Qualified Terminable Interest Property Trust (QTIP)

A new type of marital deduction trust was created with the enactment of the unlimited marital deduction in 1981. This type of trust is ideal for those wanting to provide for the support of the surviving spouse, without giving the spouse the right to give the property to unintended beneficiaries at the spouse's death, as would be the case with the power of appointment trust. A trust will qualify as a QTIP if: (a) the spouse must receive all of the income, at least annually, for the spouse's life; (b) no one, including the spouse, may have the power to appoint (transfer) the trust property away from the spouse during the spouse's lifetime; and (c) the personal representative of the deceased spouse's estate must make an appropriate election on the estate tax return of the deceased spouse. At the death of the surviving spouse, the QTIP trust distributes the balance of the trust estate to those persons named by the person creating the trust.

Qualified Domestic Trust (QDOT)

In 1988, Congress changed the tax law to disallow any marital deduction for property passing to a non-citizen spouse, unless the transfer was in the form of a QDOT for such spouse. The concern was that substantial assets would be transferred tax-free to the non-citizen spouse, who would then move out of the country, with the result that no estate tax would ever be paid on the transferred assets. To qualify as a QDOT, the trust must meet the requirements of one of the marital trust enumerated above and must have at least one trustee who is a United States citizen or is a domestic corporation. The United States trustee must have the right in the trust agreement to withhold tax on any distribution from the trust, other than distributions of income. The requirements are complicated and require trust drafting by an experienced attorney. Failure to follow the rules can result in tax disaster.

Summary

This chapter covers an extensive subject in summary form, and contains some oversimplification of the complexities experienced in estate planning for the marital deduction, or during the administration of an estate. However, a basic understanding of the fundamentals of the marital deduction is important in planning estates of married couples

THE COLORADO ESTATE TAX

The art of taxation consists in so plucking the goose as to get the most feathers with the least hissing.

— Lord Herbert Louis Samuel

For several decades, Colorado had an inheritance tax, which was a state death tax system based upon the amount of property received by a beneficiary, and the relationship of the beneficiary to the decedent. In 1980, Colorado's inheritance tax was repealed and replaced by an estate tax. Under the old inheritance tax, joint safe deposit boxes and joint bank accounts were "frozen" at death, and could only be released after approval by the Inheritance Tax Department. This procedure no longer exists.

Colorado's estate tax (sometimes called a "pick-up tax" or a "gap tax") is applicable only to estates that owe some federal estate tax. It is designed to take advantage of the credit for state death taxes that allows a certain portion of any death tax paid to a state to count as a credit against the federal estate tax. The Colorado estate tax does not cost the estate any additional taxes. If Colorado had no estate tax, there would be no credit against the federal estate tax, so what would have been a credit must then be paid to the federal government. The Colorado estate tax merely picks up the amount allowed as a credit against the federal tax. This is why the tax is often called a "pick-up tax" or a "gap tax."

Colorado will collect the maximum credit allowable if the decedent's estate is physically located entirely within Colorado's jurisdiction. A proportionate share of the credit will be claimed if the decedent dies owning property subject to the jurisdiction of more than one state.

Colorado's estate tax is administered under the direction of the Colorado Department of Revenue. This department has broad powers to insure proper enforcement of the tax, and may exchange information with the Internal Revenue Service.

A Colorado estate tax return must be filed if a federal estate tax return is required. The Colorado return must be filed within nine months of the date of death. If the return is not timely filed, there is a penalty equal to 5% of the tax due per month, up to a maximum of 25%. However, if an extension to file the federal estate tax return is granted by the Internal Revenue Service, a similar extension will be given for the Colorado return. No penalty is charged during the extension period.

In addition to the penalty for late filing, if the tax is not paid within 9 months of the date of death, it will bear interest until paid at the legal rate set from time to time by Colorado statutes.

Summary

Under the present federal estate tax laws, the amount of the state death tax credit collected by Colorado is declining. In the future, this will put financial pressure on our legislature to pass a state inheritance or estate tax to fill the economic gap. Therefore, it is important to watch developments in the area of state death taxation with the new challenges such a tax will add to the process of planning your estate.

LIFETIME GIFTS AS AN
ESTATE PLANNING STRATEGY

*Life's most persistent and urgent question is,
what are you doing for others?*
— Martin Luther King, Jr.

Lifetime gifts often play an important part in passing property from one generation to the next, even without the motivation of tax planning. Parents may transfer an interest in the family business to their children in order to increase the children's interest in the enterprise, and to equip them to assume the responsibilities of management. Farmers and ranchers often give their children a few head of livestock so that they acquire experience in animal husbandry, or have an opportunity to build a herd of their own over the years. Parents create educational accounts to provide for the future education of children or grandchildren.

In addition, gifts often have the benefit of reducing income and estate taxes, as well as lowering the costs of probate. In planning gifts, however, the continuing needs for the welfare of the person making the gift (the "donor"), and of the one receiving it (the "donee") should be carefully considered. An older person should clearly not make gifts that would impair his security, the capacity to provide for the future, or the opportunity to continue useful and gainful employment. A child should not be given funds or property which they are too young to handle, or which will impair their incentive to succeed and engage in meaningful employment. The selection and timing of gifts to young people who lack experience in financial management should be designed to further their training and development, with adequate provision for the care and management of property until they are likely to have financial maturity. The desire to affect tax savings, or to avoid probate costs, should be secondary considerations when compared the human aspect of property ownership.

There are generally three primary reasons to consider lifetime gifts. First, to give the donee financial independence or training in the prudent management of finances. Second, to reduce estate taxes by reducing the value of the donor's taxable estate (a benefit only if the total value of the donor's assets exceeds the estate tax exempt amount — see Chapter 6). Third, to benefit charitable enterprises (the "good feeling" gift).

Gifts of Appreciating Assets

One tax advantage to lifetime gift giving is that it can remove an asset with a rapidly appreciating value from the donor's estate for federal estate tax purposes. For example, if a parent gives the children real estate worth $100,000 at the time of the gift, but over the years the land appreciates in value so that it is worth $150,000 when the parent dies, then the $50,000 of appreciated value will escape taxation. If the gift had not been made, then the entire $150,000 worth of land would have been included in the parents' taxable estate. Thus, giving away assets likely to appreciate in value over the years has definite tax advantages. The more rapidly an asset is expected to appreciate in value, the more important it is to consider that asset for gifting.

The benefit of gifting appreciating assets only applies in the context of saving estate taxes. If there were no estate tax, then gifting appreciating assets suddenly becomes an income tax detriment. This is because of the tax rule that provides a "stepped-up basis" for assets transferred at death. An asset transferred during the lifetime of the property owner carries with it the income tax basis it had in the hands of the donor. Therefore, when the donee eventually sells the asset, the donor's basis is used in determining capital gain or loss for income tax purposes. However, if the property owner holds the asset until death, the beneficiary who receives the asset gets a new income tax basis equal to the asset's date of death value, and this would result in little or no income tax if the asset is sold shortly after death.

Removal of Gift Taxes from the Estate

A second tax advantage of lifetime gift giving requires an under-standing of the concept of tax-exclusive rates and tax-inclusive rates. This concept results from the different base to which gift taxes and estate taxes apply. Even though the tax rates are the same for life-time transfers and death transfers, the base to which the rate applies is different. The important difference to understand is that the estate tax is imposed on the before tax value of the assets owned by the property owner at death, and the tax is then payable out of those assets. On the other hand, the gift tax is imposed on the person mak-ing the gift (the donor) and is paid out of the donor's other property. The payment of the gift tax reduces the property owner's estate remaining at death, and, therefore, reduces the estate tax. This is a rather technical issue to understand, but accept the proposition that lifetime taxable gifts often result in overall lower transfer tax than taxable transfers at death.

The exception to this rule relates to gifts made within three years of the donor's death. To eliminate some of the planning opportunities for donor's who have limited life expectancies, the tax law requires that any gift taxes paid on gifts made by a donor or such donor's spouse within three years of the donor's death are required to be included in the donor's taxable estate at death. In spite of this rule, making gifts of rapidly appreciating assets may still be a good plan.

Contemplation-of-Death Gifts

Prior to 1982, the rule was that any gift made within three years of death was still included in the donor's taxable estate at death. However, due to a change in the law for estates of decedents dying after 1981, with certain limited exceptions, the three-year rule will no longer apply. Therefore, a taxpayer can literally make deathbed gifts of the annual gift tax exclusion amount to each of an unlimited number of family members and relatives, without gift or estate tax consequences. The major exception to this rule concerns gifts of life insurance policies within three years of the insured donor's death.

Gift Tax Annual Exclusion

A third way that gift-giving can save estate taxes is by using the annual exclusion. Currently, the annual exclusion amount is $11,000. The annual exclusion is indexed for inflation. The annual exclusion amount may be given each year to any number of people. Moreover, since most annual exclusion gifts will not be included in the donor's estate at death, all such gifts will escape both gift and estate taxation. The provision for an annual exclusion was originally included to permit normal periodic gifts, such as wedding and Christmas presents among family members and friends, without the discouraging effect of taxes. In large families, the annual exclusion offers the opportunity for substantial property transfers without tax concerns. For example, a person with four children can make gifts of up to $44,000 a year tax-free.

A married couple can each give the annual exclusion amount. With four children, a couple can gift $88,000 each year. Even if the gifted property belongs entirely to only one of the spouses, the tax law allows for "gift splitting," if the non-owner spouse consents to treat the gift as being made one-half by the non-owner spouse. Thus, if a husband and wife establish an annual gift-giving program, then over a period of 10 years they could divest themselves, tax-free, of the quite substantial sum of $880,000 worth of property. The power of annual exclusion gifting is not restricted only to children, but can be extended to spouses of children, grandchildren, extended family members, and others.

Gifts for Medical Needs and Tuition

In addition to the annual exclusion gift, a donor may make unlimited payments for tuition and medical expenses of any person. Such gifts are in addition to the $11,000 annual exclusion gifting amount, and do not reduce the estate tax exemption. More importantly, there is no limit to the amount that can be given.

Some rules apply. No surprise. Payments must be made directly to the institution providing the benefit, and not to the person receiving the benefit. Tuition must be paid to a qualified educational institution — no piano lessons. Payments are for tuition only, and do not extend to room and board, or to books.

Income Tax Savings from Gifting

Another tax advantage of lifetime gifts that must be considered is the income tax savings that may result from transferring income-producing property from a high bracket taxpayer to a low bracket taxpayer. Because of the progressive nature of the income tax, a parent may be in the top tax bracket, while children may be in substantially lower tax brackets. With substantial income-producing assets, this may save a significant amount of tax in the family. Congress is not unaware of such strategies, and has created a rule that blocks this planning technique where the children are minors. A child less than 14 years of age is generally taxed on unearned income at the parent's marginal tax rate after the first $1,300. This is referred to as the "kiddie tax" and should be discussed with your accountant before making any plans to shift income for tax purposes.

How Gift Tax Is Figured

When gifts to a single person exceed the annual exclusion, a gift tax return must be filed. The gift tax is computed on a cumulative basis, which means that the gift tax takes into consideration all past gifts. If gifts in a given year exceed the annual exclusion and the exclusion for tuition and medical expenses, the excess amount of the gift is taken as a reduction of the applicable exclusion amount discussed in Chapter 6 ($1,000,000 in 2002 and 2003). Any gifting amount in excess of the applicable exclusion amount is then taxed. When taxable gifts are made over a number of years, the amount of the tax is determined by calculating the gift tax due on an amount equal to all past and current gifts, and subtracting from it any tax paid on prior year gift tax returns. For this reason, gift tax brackets increase as taxable gifts are made.

Making Gifts to Minors

A minor cannot be named as the owner of property without creating problems. If a minor is the owner, the property cannot later be mortgaged or sold without the appointment of a court supervised conservator. This is because a minor cannot make legally binding contracts. In Colorado, a guardian is primarily the person designated to have physical custody of a minor child, and to serve in the role of a parent. This person makes decisions regarding the welfare of the designated minor child. A conservator is the person given the authority to handle the property of a minor, and to make decisions relating to investments and the management of all types of assets which the minor owns or may be entitled to receive. Conservatorship laws are designed to provide the maximum protection for the protected person. Court accountings are required, and, unless the conservator is a bank or trust company, the conservator may be required to obtain a surety bond. A conservatorship is very inflexible. There several better alternatives for ownership of property by minors.

Uniform Transfers to Minors Act

In Colorado, the property of minor may be registered in the name of an adult person or a financial institution to be held for the benefit of the minor. Title to the property is registered as "(Name of custodian) as Custodian for (Name of minor) under the Colorado Uniform Transfers to Minors Act." The custodian has authority to invest the money and use it for the education and support of the minor. There can only be a single custodian listed on the account, but a successor custodian may be named in case the initial custodian dies or resigns. When the minor reaches 21 years of age, the remaining assets are distributed to him or her. This is a very easy and flexible way to transfer property to a minor.

Irrevocable Trusts

Some parents object to having minors receive property when they reach 21 years of age. Under the Colorado Uniform Transfers to Minors Act, there is no choice but to turn the assets over at that time. Therefore, in making large gifts, an irrevocable trust may be preferable since it can be extended to whatever age the donor wants. There are several types of irrevocable trust that may be suitable for gifting purposes. These are discussed in Chapter 18.

State Tuition Programs

Gifts to state qualified tuition programs receive special tax treatment, and have become popular methods to set aside funds for the education of children and grandchildren. Contributions to such programs do not qualify for the unlimited gift tax exclusion for educational gifts, but gifts in excess of the annual exclusion amount may be treated as if made over a five year period. Therefore, it is possible to make a gift of $55,000 to a state qualified tuition plan, and have it treated as an "advance" of gifts in future years. Of course, any gift to the minor on whose behalf the fund is created in any of the next five years would have to be reported on a gift tax return, since the annual exclusion for that year would have already been used. These educational gift funds are created under Section 529 of the Internal Revenue Code, and are referred to as "529 Plans."

Summary

The desire to and the necessity for giving is a fact of life. Even so, it is sometimes difficult to convince people that it is more blessed to give than to receive. In addition, the tax laws view lifetime giving as merely a way of avoiding taxation at death. Therefore, gifts must be structured in a manner which will optimize the benefit to the recipient as well as satisfy the motivation of the donor. Large gifts require careful planning, and the advice of qualified advisors is imperative.

SHOULD I MAKE GIFTS
TO CHARITY?

You will find, as you look back upon your life,
that the moments that stand out are the moments
when you have done things for others.

— Henry Drummond

When asked about including a charitable contribution as part of
the estate plan, many simply reply, "Charity begins at home." This
attitude persists despite the undeniable fact that all of us benefit from
public organizations — often in ways we don't see. It is also a
proven statistic that most charitable organizations depend on the
public support of individual donors. A "2000 Giving USA" study
shows the following pattern of charitable contributions: 75.6% individuals, 10.4% foundations, 8.2% bequests, and 5.8% businesses.

What are our favorite charitable causes? The Denver Foundation
conducted an extensive "2000 Giving and Volunteering Study"
which examined many facets of charitable giving in Metro Denver.
The most popular cause for contributions is helping people who are
in need, such as the poor, hungry, or homeless. At the other end of
the giving spectrum, arts and cultural organizations received the
least number of gifts.

Although the "2000 Giving and Volunteering Study" reports that nine-out-of-ten (90%) of persons in Metro Denver give something to charity, donations have not kept pace with income growth. In 2000, Metro Denver residents gave approximately 2.5% of their income. The "Study" indicates the following key attributes of those who are the most like to give:

- *Volunteerism* – Those who volunteer their services to non-profit organizations are likely to also contribute their dollars.
- *Religion* – Those who rate religion as "very important" tended to donate more than those who did not rate religion as important to their lives.
- *Family Culture* – Those with a family history of giving tended to give more often than those where training in philanthropy was absent.

The decision to make gifts to charity, either during one's lifetime or by will, is a personal matter. Obviously, the selection of the charity, the timing, the amount, and the type of property given will depend upon the individual's attitude, desires, financial resources, and responsibilities.

Once the decision has been made to contribute to charity, or at least to consider it, the tax effects of the gift become important. The tax laws are intended to encourage philanthropy. Income, gift, and estate tax deductions are allowable for certain charitable gifts. If a person can accomplish his charitable objectives and reduce tax liabilities in the process, we can learn what it means to be a "cheerful giver."

Gifts of Cash or Property

When considering a charitable contribution by will, most people think in terms of a cash bequest of a fixed amount, with the bulk of the estate passing to the surviving spouse and children. Under such circumstances the entire amount of the charitable bequest is usually deductible for federal estate tax purposes.

Often, however, cash will be needed by the estate to defray costs of administration and taxes. Payment of the charitable legacies in cash could produce a cash shortage, necessitating the sale of other assets. The estate may be composed primarily of real estate or closely held corporate stocks, which may be non-liquid in the sense that they cannot be sold easily. Sale of those properties, either to pay the charitable cash bequest or to restore the cash used to pay the charity, may not only be inconvenient, but may result in an income tax if the property sold has appreciated in value between the date of the decedent's death and the time of the sale. To avoid these problems, the individual may wish to leave property to charity instead of cash. The entire value of the property given will usually be estate tax deductible.

Fixed Amount or Percentage?

Instead of giving a specific dollar amount or designated properties to charity, one may wish to consider giving a fixed percentage of the estate. If the will is drafted so that administrative costs of the estate do not come out of the gift, the entire gift will be deductible for federal estate tax purposes. Another advantage of the percentage gift is an across-the-board reduction of the gift if the estate has a lower value than the donor expected.

Income Tax Deduction for Gifts

There are limitations on the amount of charitable gifts that are income tax deductible in a given year. In addition, the deduction will vary with the type of property donated. Generally, contributions of cash to public charities are deductible up to 50% of the contribution base, which is adjusted gross income, subject to certain adjustments. However, the same contribution to certain private family charitable foundations is deductible up to only 30% of the contribution base. The size of the charitable contribution in any particular year must be carefully planned if the donor intends the entire contribution to be tax deductible. The amount of the donation to a public charity that exceeds the income tax limitations can be deducted in the five following years. Alternatively, the donations can be made over a period of years. Thus, rather than giving a block of stock in one particular year, a smaller number of shares might be given over several years. Similarly, undivided interests in real estate can be given periodically to maximize available income tax benefits. Not all assets will qualify for the 50% deduction. It is important to seek qualified tax advice before making large gifts.

Gifts of Life Insurance

There are, of course, other methods of making charitable contributions. One of these involves using life insurance. An individual may transfer to a charity an existing life insurance policy and be entitled to a charitable deduction based on the value of the policy. Subsequent premium payments will also be deductible for income tax purposes. If the donor keeps the policy, but names the charity as beneficiary, the proceeds are includable in the taxable estate at death (because the policy was owned by the deceased insured), but an estate tax charitable deduction would be allowed.

Charitable Remainder Trusts

Most of us have the erroneous idea that being a philanthropist requires that we must always end up economically poorer after making a gift to charity. This may be true with respect to an outright gift since the donated property and the donor have permanently parted ways. However, in a deferred-giving transaction that uses a charitable remainder trust, the donor transfers property to a trust, reserves an annuity interest in the property for life, and contributes the remainder interest in the property to the charity at the donor's death. This type of arrangement can have income, gift, and estate tax benefits.

Formation

Let's look at the basic requirements for a trust to qualify as a charitable remainder trust. These rules are set forth in regulations issued by the IRS. There are several forms of a charitable remainder trust. In the discussion which follows, we will address the "standard" charitable remainder trust.

- The trust must pay a fixed percentage (not less than 5%) of the net fair market value of its assets to the beneficiary.
- The payment of the fixed percentage amount must be made at least annually.
- The fixed percentage is based upon the net fair market value of the trust assets at the beginning of each year.
- The payment must be made for either a term of years (not to exceed 20 years) or for the life or lives of named individuals. For example, payments can be made to a husband and wife during their joint lives, and then to the survivor for life.
- When the last beneficiary dies, the payments stop and the remainder of the trust is then transferred to one or more designated charitable organizations.

Initial Tax Consequences

There is an immediate income tax charitable deduction when the trust is created. The amount of the deduction is the value of the charity's right to receive the trust principal after the last beneficiary's death. This amount is determined by actuarial tables published by the Internal Revenue Service, and is based on the age of the beneficiary at the time the trust is created.

Gifts to a charitable remainder trust are deductible up to 50% of the donor's adjusted gross income if the trust is funded with money, and the charitable beneficiary is a school, church, hospital or other public charity. When stocks are contributed, the deduction is usually limited to 30% of the donor's adjusted gross income. However, if the entire amount of the deduction cannot be fully used in the year of the contribution to the trust, the excess may be deducted over the five following years.

There is no capital gain tax upon the transfer of appreciated property to fund a charitable remainder trust. If the trust subsequently sells the appreciated property, there is no tax to the trust since the assets are ultimately payable to a tax-exempt organization. Therefore, income is generated from investment of the full fair market value of the transferred assets without dilution for any income tax which would have been paid on the capital appreciation if the asset had been sold outside the trust.

Example of Economics

Consider the following example which describes a situation in which the use of a charitable remainder trust might be particularly advantageous. John Philanthropist has $1,000,000 worth of stock in the Widget Company which he purchased when it was just getting started in business. The total cost of the stock was originally only $50,000. Since the Widget Company is still an aggressive growth firm, it reinvests most of its profits in research and development. As a result, the company only pays a modest 1% dividend, and in some years no dividend at all is paid. John Philanthropist is in his retirement years and is looking for safe investments which will yield a secure and predictable income to him. The Widget Company certainly no longer meets these qualifications. In addition, John wants to diversify his investment so that his financial future is not dependent on a single stock. However, John does not want to sell the stock because of the tremendous capital gains tax that would result. Therefore, although John may be rich in property, he is cash poor and locked into an investment that no longer meets his needs.

John could solve his problem by creating a charitable remainder trust. He would transfer the appreciated securities of the Widget Company to the trust in exchange for a lifetime income payment of 8% of the value of the trust assets. There would be no capital gain upon transfer of the stock to the trust. The trustee would sell the stock because it would not be concerned about capital gains tax since it is not a taxable entity. The trust would reinvest the proceeds from the sale.

In the first year, John Philanthropist would receive $80,000 from the trust ($1,000,000 x 8%). Let's assume that one year later, because of good investment decisions made by the trustee, the trust assets are worth $1,100,000. Since the trust percentage is calculated each year based upon the current fair market value of the trust assets, John would receive $80,800 for the second year ($1,100,000 x 8%). If the assets are worth $1,200,000 at the beginning of the next year, John will receive $90,600 for that year ($1,200,000 x 8%). As long as the trust assets continue to appreciate in value, the annual payments to John would similarly increase. In addition, John would receive an income tax deduction in the year the trust is created. The amount of the deduction would depend upon his age at the time of the creation of the trust and the value of the assets contributed to the trust. Depending upon the size of the charitable deduction, some portion of it might be carried over to future years to protect income in those years.

Continuing Income Tax Treatment

It is important to understand how the income from a charitable remainder trust is taxed to the recipient. There is a four-tier distribution system which determines the taxability of trust distributions. First, each trust payment is treated as ordinary income to the extent of the trust's ordinary income for the year of the trust distribution and any undistributed ordinary income from prior years. Second, if the trust payment to the beneficiary exceeds the current and accumulated ordinary income earned by the trust, the excess is taxed as capital gain to the extent the trust has capital gains for the current year and undistributed capital gain from prior years. If a trust payment is greater than the current and accumulated ordinary income and capital gains of the trust, other forms of trust income, such as tax-exempt income for the current and prior years, are treated as taxable distributions to the beneficiary. After all of the above amounts have been exhausted, any trust distribution will be treated as a tax-free return of capital.

Illustration 9-1 demonstrates how charitable remainders trust works.

Illustration 9-1

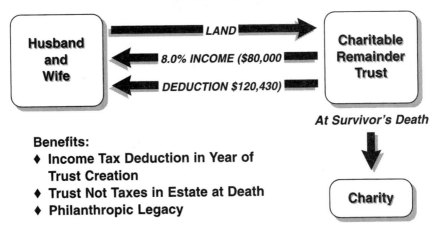

Tax Benefits

Benefits:
- ♦ **Income Tax Deduction in Year of Trust Creation**
- ♦ **Trust Not Taxes in Estate at Death**
- ♦ **Philanthropic Legacy**

The Wealth Replacement Trust

A concern of some donors is the fact that the assets transferred to the charitable remainder trust will pass to the charity at the donor's death and diminish the value of the estate passing to children or other family members. If this is a concern, many donors create an irrevocable life insurance trust, which applies for and owns a life insurance policy on the donor in an amount equal to the value of the property transferred to the charitable trust. (See Chapter 19 for additional information regarding life insurance trusts.) In many cases, the increased cash flow from the charitable remainder trust, together with the income tax savings generated by the gift, are more than sufficient to pay the premiums on the life insurance policy. The irrevocable life insurance trust will keep the death benefit out of the donor's taxable estate for federal estate tax purposes. Therefore, the life insurance trust provides a tax-free replacement of the property eventually passing to the charity.

Charitable Lead Trusts (The Boomerang Gift)

You Had a Dream

Imagine this. You have a dream that your tax advisor has revealed to you a secret strategy in which you are able to make a substantial tax-free gift that pays an annuity to your favorite charity for many years. Each year the charity acknowledges your generosity with a dinner with your favorite professor, football tickets, and perhaps even putting your name on a brass plaque somewhere for posterity to see. Then you dream that years later the charity returns the gift to your children, but it has grown and is now two or three times larger than when you started — and your children receive the enlarged gift completely tax-free. Thus, the gift you made turned into a boomerang. It did a good work and then returned to your family.

This is no dream. The strategy is no secret. There is a tool that has been used by knowledgeable tax planners for years to accomplish these objectives. It is called the Charitable Lead Annuity Trust (CLAT).

The Jackie O. Zero Tax Plan

Although the CLAT has been an accepted tax planning strategy for years, it gained notoriety when it was reported that Jacqueline Kennedy Onassis had included such a trust in her Last Will and Testament to transfer her estimated estate of $120 million to her grandchildren without significant estate tax consequences.

Here is how the plan was to work. After some specific gifts to various family members, the balance of Mrs. Onassis's estate was to be transferred to the trustee of a CLAT to be called "The C & J Foundation." The trust was to pay a designated annuity to charities selected by the trustees for 24 years. At the end of the trust term, the remaining assets were to be distributed to Mrs. Onassis's grandchildren.

Let's examine this strategy in more detail. Upon creation of the trust, there were two sets of beneficiaries established. First, there was the charity to the extent of its annuity. This portion would be tax-exempt as a charitable transfer. Second, there was a gift to the grandchildren of the remainder of the trust at the end of the charitable interest. This interest would be taxable to the extent it exceeded the applicable estate tax exemption. Each of these two separate interests had to be valued using IRS tables.

As it turned out, due to the careful calculations of Mrs. Onassis's attorneys, the value of the right of the charity to receive the designated annuity for 22 years was equal to almost the entire value of the estate. Therefore, the value of the grandchildren's right to receive the trust remainder 24 years later was negligible.

Illustration 9-2 shows the outline of a charitable lead trust.

Illustration 9-2

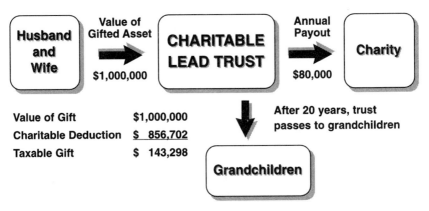

Value of Gift	$1,000,000	
Charitable Deduction	$ 856,702	
Taxable Gift	$ 143,298	

Tax-Free Wealth Accumulation

In the right circumstances, the power of the CLAT cannot be overstated. By picking the proper amount to pay the charity, and the correct number of years during which this annuity to the charity is paid, it is possible to zero-out the gift and estate tax on an unlimited amount of wealth. Although the Jacqueline Kennedy Onassis CLAT was created by her Last Will and Testament, a donor can create a CLAT during his lifetime. The benefit of a CLAT is greatly magnified when the property transferred to the trust is expected to rapidly appreciate in value over the term of the trust. For example, assume the annual payment to the charity is set at 8%, but the trust assets are growing at the rate of 12% annually. The growth of the trust assets over and above the amount paid annually to the charity keeps accumulating in the trust for eventual distribution to the children or grandchildren. Since the gift or estate tax consequences of the CLAT are determined as of the date of death for a testamentary trust, and as of the date of the gift for a lifetime trust, the actual value of the assets at the end of the CLAT is immaterial for tax purposes.

To understand the power of a CLAT, let's examine a 20 year trust funded with $1 million of assets. The charity is to receive an 8% annuity. It is anticipated that the assets will grow at a rate of 12% (representing the combined income earned on the assets and capital appreciation). The charity receives $80,000 each year for 20 years. At the end of the CLAT (at the end of the 20 year term), using the tables and interest rates in effect at the time of this writing, the donor's children will receive $3,882,098 tax-free. All the children must do is wait for a few years before they will have the property to enjoy. However, if the trust is established when the children are young, they may receive the property out of the trust just at the time they need it to start a business, or invest in some other worthwhile endeavor.

Annuity Trust vs. Unitrust

The annual payment to the charity can take the form of either an annuity or a unitrust amount. An annuity trust pays a specific amount of money as set forth in the trust agreement. The annuity amount may be a stated dollar amount, or it may be an amount equal to a stated percent of the initial value of the contribution to the trust. A unitrust pays a different amount each year equal to a fixed percentage of net fair market value of the trust assets as determined annually on a designated date. The annuity trust is usually preferred because it produces a larger tax-free gift to the children.

Income Tax Consequences

For income tax purposes, the CLAT may be classified as either a grantor trust or a non-grantor trust. With the grantor CLAT, the tax-payer contributing the property to the trust (called the grantor) is considered to be the owner of the trust assets and is, therefore, taxed on the current income of the trust each year. However, to the extent the income is paid out to the charitable beneficiary, the grantor may take a charitable deduction. The grantor also receives an income tax deduction when assets are transferred to the trust equal to the value of the charity's income interest determined under the prescribed IRS tables.

With the non-grantor CLAT, the grantor is not treated as the owner of the trust assets and is not taxed on the trust income. Instead, the trust is taxed on the income to the extent such income is not distributed to the charity each year. There is no charitable deduction for the contribution to a non-grantor CLAT. Most CLATs are designed as non-grantor trusts.

Gift Tax Consequences

A gift tax deduction is allowed for the value of the charity's income interest. Remember, this value is determined using the IRS tables. A gift tax return must be filed in the year that property is transferred to the trust. After the initial contribution to the trust, no further contributions can be made. If the value of the charitable income interest does not equal the full value of the contribution, the resulting gift to the children of the remainder interest does not qualify for the annual gift tax exclusion.

Selection of the Trustee

Some versions of the CLAT may allow the grantor to also be the trustee. However, caution should be exercised in this regard, and it is usually best if an independent trustee is selected. This is especially important if the charitable beneficiary is a private family foundation.

Compounding the Leverage

The greater the amount of assets which can be transferred to the CLAT without gift tax consequences, the greater the amount eventually distributed tax-free to the children. A popular device to accomplish this goal is the family limited partnership. Appreciating assets are transferred to a family limited partnership. Restricted limited partnership units are used for gifting to the CLAT. These limited partnership units have no public market in which they can be sold, and because of the limitations placed on the units, they make highly undesirable investments to anyone outside the family. Therefore, the value of the units can be discounted for gifting purposes. This allows for a greater amount of underlying asset values to be transferred to the CLAT.

The tax laws offer few opportunities to do well by doing good. This is one of those opportunities which, in the proper circumstances, can allow you to get the lifetime satisfaction of seeing your charitable goals accomplished without sacrificing your children's inheritance.

Private Charitable Foundations

If a donor wishes to make substantial gifts to charity, the family might consider establishing their own private charitable foundation. Usually an individual establishes a foundation in the form of a nonprofit corporation, but an irrevocable trust may also be used. A private foundation receives contributions from family members, and makes grants to other public charitable organizations as determined each year by the family members who form the board of trustees. In order to gain tax-exempt status, the foundation must file an application with the IRS within fifteen months after it is formed. If a favorable ruling is obtained, subsequent gifts to the foundation are deductible for income, gift, and estate tax purposes, and the income of the foundation, with certain exceptions, is tax-exempt.

Some of the primary reasons people create family foundations are to maintain control over the charitable investments and to direct the focus of the family charitable giving. Since the donation is not given to a specific charity, the family trustees can change the direction of the giving each year. The family philanthropic interests can be memorialized and perpetuated for years in the future. Children and grandchildren can be guided in the development of their civic responsibilities.

There are, however, disadvantages to forming a private foundation. First, the amount of charitable deduction allowed for gifts to private foundations is more limited than for gifts to public charities. The IRS requires private foundations to maintain strict records, and file complicated tax forms each year. Since the private foundation is a separate corporation, annual meetings of the trustees must be held. A private foundation must make minimum distributions of at least 5% of the value of the foundation's assets each year. Although generally tax-exempt, a private foundation must pay a 2% excise tax on all "net investment income" of the foundation.

Obviously, a private foundation is not for everyone. However, it may fit certain families. An increasingly popular alternative to the private foundation is the donor advised fund, created in conjunction with a specific public charity or with a community foundation.

Donor Advised Funds

A donor advised fund may be created with a community foundation. In Colorado, there are a number of community foundations serving various regions throughout the state. A separate fund designated by the name of the donor is established in a written agreement with the community foundation. This agreement specifies the particular uses for distributions from the fund, and may nominate family members to be consulted prior to distributions being made. Usually, only the income of the fund is distributed each year, and the principal of the fund continues as a permanent endowment honoring the family. The benefits of this form of charitable planning include:

professional investment management by the community foundation advisors, elimination of private foundation tax returns and corporate reporting requirements, assistance with researching the background and effectiveness of charitable organizations to which grants are made, and continued family involvement in the giving process.

Gift of Remainder Interest in Personal Residence

This gifting strategy may be characterized as the gift you get to keep. The donor contributes a personal residence, farm, vacation home, or stock in a cooperative apartment used as a residence, to a charity. However, the donor retains the right to continue to live in the residence for a specified term of years, or may continue to occupy it for the rest of the donor's lifetime. The donor is entitled to an immediate income tax deduction based on the value of the remainder interest in the residence contributed to charity. The value of the remainder interest is computed using actuarial tables published by the IRS. If the residence is sold during the donor's lifetime, the consent of the charity would be required. After a sale of the residence, the donor would continue to have a life estate in the sale proceeds. If the donor makes improvements to the residence, there will be an additional charitable deduction for the charitable remainder interest. At the death of the donor, the property will belong to the charity.

Pooled Income Funds

A pooled income fund is similar in concept to a mutual fund. These funds are offered by many charities in Colorado. A donor generally contributes cash or securities to the fund, and receives a pro rata share of the fund's income for the rest of the donor's life. Upon the donor's death, the donor's interest in the fund is then given to the charity. If appreciated stock is used to make the contribution, the donor not only receives an immediate charitable income tax deduction, but also avoids any income tax on the appreciation in the securities contributed. The fund managers diversify the fund's investments and attempt to maximize the return. Therefore, a pooled income fund permits the donor with highly appreciated, but low-yielding stock, to diversify and increase the income received, while paying no tax on the capital gain and receiving a current income tax deduction.

Gift Annuities

Many charities are licensed in Colorado to sell gift annuities. The donor transfers money or property to the charity in exchange for the annuity. The donor receives a guaranteed fixed sum, usually monthly, commencing either immediately or at a future date, and continuing for the rest of the donor's life, and, if desired, for the life of the donor's spouse. The donor receives a charitable income tax deduction and favored treatment on any capital gain in the property transferred to the charity. The older the donor, the higher the rate of interest used in computing the annuity. A charitable annuity is guaranteed, and is an excellent supplement to Social Security and other retirement benefits. The disadvantage is the loss of the asset used to purchase the annuity, meaning the donor should not give all investigable assets in exchange for an annuity since this would eliminate the ability to invade the principal if unanticipated financial needs arise in later years.

Summary

Charitable giving is a learned behavior. It is in the homes of America that we begin to instill our children with a sense of obligation for the needs of others and with a sense that rock concerts are not cultural events. Only when the importance of the world outside our own little kingdom is acknowledged will the importance of charitable institutions be esteemed. However, there is nothing wrong with structuring charitable giving, when possible, to provide tax benefits to the donor. Those who have been especially blessed with worldly possessions will find in this chapter several methods for accomplishing both tax benefits and fulfillment of social responsibility.

SHOULD I MAKE A WILL?

Then he said, "This is what I'll do. I will tear down my
barns and build
bigger ones, and there I will store all my grain and my
goods. And I'll
say to myself, 'You have plenty of good things laid up for
many years.
Take life easy; eat, drink and be merry.'" But God said
to him, "You fool.
This very night your life will be demanded from you. Then
who will get
what you have prepared for yourself?"
— Gospel of Luke 12:18-20

Most people work hard to acquire and keep property during their lifetimes. However, a surprisingly large number of people die without a will. Studies conducted by various trust companies and the American Bar association indicate that only 20% of Americans have wills. Those who do not have a will forfeit the right to determine the disposition of their property, and fail to make informed decisions to provide for their family's continued well-being. They die leaving the security of their family to chance, and the disposition of their property to the law.

Why do so few people take the time to prepare a will? Studies indicate several reasons: discomfort with talking about a subject associated with dying, concern about the cost of the lawyer, uncertainty regarding the best manner of passing property to a spouse and children, and disagreement between spouses on how to treat children (especially in multiple marriage situations). But the most important reason people fail to plan properly is procrastination.

To avoid leaving the distribution of your estate to chance, consider the following recommendations. First, realize that you are never too young to think about having a will. Second, ask your financial advisor or banker for the recommendation of a lawyer who specializes in estate planning matters. Third, ask the lawyer if the initial consultation is complementary and if not, what the charge would be (most estate planning lawyers will give you the first meeting without charge). Fourth, make certain you understand the planning alternatives the lawyer recommends (never accept a recommendation you don't understand — if the lawyer can't explain it to you, it probably doesn't make sense for you to attempt it). Fifth, find out how the lawyer charges, and what the recommended plan will cost (many estate planning lawyers will quote you a flat fee so there are no surprises). Finally, ask how soon the documents will be ready for you to review and execute. If you follow these steps, much of the mystery and fear will be eliminated.

Who Can and Should Make a Will?

The records of the probate courts in Colorado show that wealthy people usually recognize the value of planning their estate. Most of the persons who die without a will are the owners of modest or medium-sized estates. Yet, saving a dollar in a small estate means much more to that family than saving a dollar would to a family with a $1 million estate.

A will is a written instrument by which a person (called a testator) disposes of that person's property — effective at death. A will is always subject to change by the testator during lifetime, and conveys no present interest in property or rights to any beneficiary until the testator's death. As a result, a will can dispose of property acquired either before or after the will is made.

Colorado law gives to every person of sound mind, who is at least 18 years old, the right to make a will. This right carries with it the privilege of disposing of one's estate in any manner and to anyone. Colorado law does not require that property be left to one's children, parents, or any other person. However, a spouse may not be disinherited unless the spouse has signed a valid waiver of his marital property rights (usually in the form of a prenuptial agreement). In the absence of a prenuptial agreement, the disinherited spouse may elect to take against the will and receive one half of the "augmented estate" of the deceased spouse. The augmented estate includes the probate estate, plus certain lifetime transfers and transfers of property not controlled by the will, such as property held in joint tenancy.

Types of Wills

There are basically two types of wills provided for by Colorado law. The most common type is the typewritten will, usually prepared by an attorney. For such a will to be valid it must be executed with certain formalities (see Chapter 12 for the requirements of a valid will).

If the requirements for execution of the will and its attestation are not strictly complied with, the will is invalid and may be contested. Likewise, if the maker is not of sound mind, or is acting under undue influence when the will is executed, the will is invalid. Hence, it is advisable to have an attorney supervise the making and execution of a will to make certain all of the prerequisites for validity and the various formalities of execution have been satisfied.

A "self-proved will" is one in which the signatures of the testator and witnesses are notarized, in addition to the other formal requirements for valid execution. This feature allows the will to be admitted to probate at the death of the testator in a formal probate proceeding without the testimony of the witnesses. A will is not invalid if it does not have this self-proving feature, but the admission of the will to probate may be more difficult.

The other type of will valid in Colorado is one in which the signature and the material provisions are written wholly in the handwriting of, and signed by, the testator. This is called a "holographic" will and does not require witnesses in order to be valid. A typewritten instrument, or one written by someone other than the maker, is not a holographic will and must be properly executed and witnessed.

Dying Without a Will

When a person dies in Colorado without a will it is referred to as dying "intestate." The laws of intestate succession determine who shall inherit the decedent's property, and in what proportions the property shall be distributed. These laws also govern the distribution of property not disposed of by a decedent's will, either because the will does not cover all of the property, or because the will is invalid. Where there is a will, unless a contrary intention is plainly expressed or necessarily implied, it will be presumed that the testator intended to dispose of the testator's entire estate according to its terms.

The decedent's separate property and the decedent's one-half interest in any community property are the only properties disposed of by a decedent's will, or by the laws of intestate succession. (Colorado is not a community property state. For more on this subject, see Chapter 16). Property owned with another person in joint tenancy passes automatically to the surviving joint owner by operation of law, regardless of the provisions in the decedent's will or the laws of intestate succession. The will also has no effect on retirement plans, life insurance payable to a named beneficiary, or on property in a revocable living trust.

The laws of intestate succession are inflexible, and are an attempt by the legislature to decide what a person would have done if the person had taken the opportunity to express his desires in a will. The rules are complex and no attempt will be made to set out all the possible alternatives, but a few examples will be instructive.

If the decedent is survived by a spouse and by children who are also the only children of the surviving spouse, the entire estate is distributed to the surviving spouse. However, if the surviving spouse has children by the marriage to the decedent and also has children by a prior marriage, then the surviving spouse only receives the first $150,000 of assets, and one-half of the balance of the assets, with the decedent's children receiving the remaining one-half of the assets. An even more unusual result occurs if the decedent has no children, but is survived by a spouse and parents — in this situation, the surviving spouse receives the first $200,000 and three-fourths of the balance of the assets, and the decedent's parents receive the other one-fourth. These examples point out the importance of having a will expressing your desires for the distribution of your assets at death.

When minor children survive a parent, the problems presented by dying without a will are particularly acute. The surviving spouse is obligated to support the children, and often is required to do so out of his own property and earnings, even though the children may have substantial inheritances of their own. Where a minor receives property through inheritance, it is usually necessary to have a conservator appointed, not only to protect the minor's property rights, but also to facilitate payment of funds to the minor. Insurance companies and governmental agencies, such as the Social Security Administration and the Veterans Administration, may require a conservatorship before they will pay funds to a minor beneficiary. Where a minor inherits an interest in real estate, title companies and lending agencies will require that a conservatorship be established before the minor's interest can be sold.

The complications are potentially even greater when an unmarried person without children dies intestate. The Colorado statute then distributes the estate to the closest living blood relative. In some cases, this may be a remote cousin who is relatively a stranger to the decedent.

Conservatorship — The Penalty of Dying Without a Will

The administration of the minor's property under a conservatorship is highly restricted, costly, and subject to court supervision to safeguard the minor's rights. The minor's money can be invested only in authorized investments, and the conservator's expenditures are also regulated. The court may insist that the conservator post a bond, with sureties as it may specify, conditioned upon the faithful discharge of the conservator's duties, all at the expense of the minor's estate. Additionally, the conservator is entitled to reasonable compensation from the estate with court approval.

When the minor reaches age 18, the conservator must deliver the minor's property to the minor regardless of the maturity or business experience of the minor. The minor is entitled to a full accounting from the conservator as to the handling of the minor's property during the entire period of the conservatorship, and should the minor be displeased with the results of the accounting, litigation may follow.

One of the unique advantages of making a will is the opportunity for the parent or grandparent to establish a trust to administer the minor's property. Such a trust will avoid the necessity of a conservatorship, and allows the maker to prescribe their own rules for the management of the trust funds, how and for what purposes the money is to be spent, and who is to be the trustee. In addition, the trust can continue beyond the time the child reaches 18 years of age to allow for the development of maturity and experience in the management of property before it is distributed. Further, the final distribution need not be all at once, but can be made in installments, enabling the child to assume responsibility in stages.

Dying Without a Will — Who Handles the Estate?

If a personal representative is not named in a will, the court will appoint a personal representative from a list of persons with priority under Colorado law. The duties of the personal representative (in some states called "executor" if there is a will, and "administrator" if there is no will) are to locate all of the property of the decedent; manage and preserve it during the period of administration; publish a notice to the decedent's creditors; pay all debts, taxes, and costs of administration; and distribute what is left according to the will or the laws of intestate succession. In the absence of a will, the personal representative appointed by the court may or may not be the person the decedent would have selected for the job. The court might not even appoint the surviving spouse or a member of the decedent's family. By making a will, the testator can choose the person best qualified to do to the job.

Each Spouse Should Have a Will

It is important for each spouse to have a will. Failure to properly plan the estates of both spouses may result in unnecessary expenses being incurred. Additionally, failure to properly plan both spouses estates may cause the loss of the opportunity to enjoy significant tax benefits which may be taken advantage of only by suitable planning while both spouses are alive. Prudent estate planning dictates that the problems of dying without a will be addressed for both spouses. One will alone does only half the job of planning for the family.

Dying with an Outdated Will

Colorado law makes special provisions for children born or adopted after the execution of a will by their parent. Those children receive a share in the estate equal in value to that which they would have received if the parent died without a will, unless: (a) it appears from the will that the omission was intentional; (b) when the will was executed the parent had one or more children and devised substantially all of his estate to the other parent of the omitted children; or (c) the parent provided for the omitted children by transfers outside the will and it is shown that the transfers were intended to be in lieu of a provision in the will.

If a person marries after signing a will, but fails to provide for a new spouse, the omitted spouse is entitled to receive the same share of the estate as if the decedent left no will, unless it appears from the will that the omission was intentional, or the decedent provided for the spouse by transfer outside the will and it is shown that the transfer was in lieu of a provision in the will. Also, remember that the surviving spouse has a right to take against the will, unless there was a prenuptial agreement.

Divorce — Its Effect on a Will

A divorce by the maker of a will affects the provisions of the will. It automatically eliminates from the will of each divorced spouse all provisions affecting the other spouse, unless the will expressly provides otherwise, or the maker remarries the former spouse. If a person is divorced and dies before remarrying and updating the will, the portion of the estate designated to go to the former spouse will not pass to the former spouse. Rather, this portion of the estate will be distributed as if the spouse failed to survive the testator.

Everyone Should Have an Up-to-Date Will

Even though a person has a properly drawn will that is kept in a place where it can be found at his death, it will be of little value to the beneficiaries if it is not up-to-date. Parenthood, grandparenthood, divorce, changing needs of beneficiaries, change of residence, sale or other disposal of property mentioned in the will, unavailability of a named personal representative or trustee, gifts, newly acquired assets, and a change in the size of the estate are all indications that the will needs to be reviewed by the maker's lawyer. An out-of-date will that no longer fits the maker's desires or the needs of the beneficiaries is little better than no will at all.

Dying without a will rarely, if ever, provides a satisfactory substitute for the making of a will. Without a will, a person has no choice as to who will administer the estate, who will be the guardian or custodian of the estate of minor children, or who will receive the property, in what proportions, and when. A will assures the maker that the property goes to the persons desired and in the desired manner. The testator can name a personal representative of the estate, a guardian, a custodian, or a trustee. A will also allows the testator to choose the sources from which debts, expenses of administration, and taxes are to be paid. Further, it can save money in court costs, guardian's fees, conservator's fees, and attorney's fees. But even more important are the savings to the family in time, worry, and court appearances, and the assurance to them that the testator planned for their continued well-being. A will, very often, is the most important legal document that a person ever executes. It, therefore, deserves thoughtful consideration and skillful preparation.

Summary

A carefully prepared will containing all of the provisions necessary to transmit property from the testator to the intended beneficiaries can be a real legacy in itself. Such a will relieves the surviving family of the many problems created by an improperly prepared will or no will at all. It seems, then, that each thoughtful man and woman owes a duty to his or her family to have a carefully prepared will in keeping with present family circumstances.

WHAT SHOULD MY WILL CONTAIN?

A well-drafted will is tailored to the individual needs and circumstances of the person who signs it (the "testator"). An ideal provision in the will of one person might be unfit, and even dangerous, if used in the will of another. Nevertheless, there are numerous provisions that are included in most wills, as well as various problems that should be considered in drafting any will.

Introductory Provisions

A will should set forth the county and state of residence of the testator. A new will does not revoke a prior will unless the new will either contains an express revocation, or contains wholly inconsistent provisions. Therefore, the testator should state his intent regarding revocation in the will.

Appointment of a Personal Representative

A personal representative is a person, bank, or trust company designated to carry out the instructions in a will, pay the debts, and protect and manage the property until it can be delivered to the beneficiaries. A will may nominate a single personal representative, or designate two or more persons or corporations to serve jointly as co-personal representatives. The personal representative does not have to live in Colorado to be eligible to serve. If the will does not nominate a personal representative, Colorado law sets forth an order of priority of persons who may be appointed as personal representative. However, if there is an objection to a person having priority for appointment, the court will appoint a personal representative that all of the beneficiaries under the will or heirs under the laws of intestacy jointly designate, or the court will select someone to serve as personal representative. To avoid the costs of a court appointment and insure that someone the testator trusts will handle the property, the testator should appoint a personal representative. It is also desirable that the will name one or more alternate personal representatives in case the person first named as personal representative or alternate personal representative is unable or unwilling to serve.

If requested by a person having an interest in the estate, and if the court agrees that it is desirable, the probate court may require that the person named as personal representative furnish a bond to guarantee the faithful performance of all duties. The cost of such a bond will be paid out of the testator's estate. If a testator desires to avoid this cost, it should be specified in the will that the personal representative need not give bond. Consideration should also be given to the matter of the personal representative's compensation for services. The will may state whether the personal representative is to serve without compensation, or is to be paid some specific amount or in some particular manner.

Provision for Payment of Debts and Taxes

Even if a will does not contain instructions to pay debts and taxes of the testator, a personal representative has a general duty to do so. Nevertheless, wills ordinarily contain such instructions, and there is value in this because the testator can spell out his exact wishes about debts and taxes. If, for example, the testator is making installment mortgage payments on a home, the will should state whether the personal representative is to pay off the mortgage in full upon the testator's death, or if the property is to be transferred to the beneficiary subject to the mortgage so that the beneficiary has the obligation to make future payments. If continuing the installment payments is desired, the will should say so.

Regarding tax payments, the testator may intend that certain property will be inherited tax-free, with the taxes paid out of other property in the estate, or the testator may want the person receiving the property to pay a portion of the death taxes. A will should address this issue rather than leaving it for the personal representative or the courts to determine.

Provisions Disposing of the Property

The principal provisions in most wills are those which set forth to whom, and in what manner, the testator's property shall pass upon death. In some states the law requires that a married person leave a specified proportion of his estate to the spouse, and the courts will give such property to the spouse even if the will does not so provide. Colorado does have this requirement. However, a spouse may waive this right during lifetime by a valid marital property agreement. Other than a spouse, a testator may leave his property to anyone — whether related or not — for a good reason, a bad reason, or no reason at all.

Likewise, a testator has great freedom of choice in determining how property shall be distributed to the persons named in the will. The testator can give the property outright; can put the property in a trust; or can give the property on condition that the person receiving it do, or refrain from doing, whatever the testator specifies. Similarly, the testator can provide that the person receiving the property is to enjoy it only during that person's lifetime (or for a certain period of time), and that thereafter the property will go to another.

There are certain technical restrictions upon a testator's power to dispose of property by will. For example, a testator must not try to control the property for too long, and he must not direct that it be used for an unlawful purpose, or for a purpose that violates so-called "public policy." However, subject only to such restrictions, a testator can, and should, have the will written so that the property will be disposed of in the exact manner desired. The aim of the lawyer who writes the will should be to find out what the testator wants to do with the property and then to word the will so that it carries out those desires as fully as possible, keeping in mind tax consequences.

Because a testator has such wide latitude in determining how the provisions of a will are to be written, only a few general comments are necessary. First and foremost, the will should be written so that it covers all of the testator's property. If this is not done, costly court proceedings may be necessary regarding the omitted property. To guard against an omission, a will should always contain a catchall provision which provides that all property of every kind that has not been specifically disposed of by other portions of the will shall be distributed in a specified manner.

The pattern of many wills is to direct that specific pieces of property, or sums of money, shall go to certain persons, and then to follow up these "specific bequests" with a general bequest, in which the rest of the property (the "residue") is left to others. Thus, a testator may give a shotgun to a friend, a sum of money to a faithful employee or charity, a farm to a certain relative, and so on, with those portions of the will being followed up by a general provision giving the residue of the estate to a spouse or children.

Colorado allows the personal effects of the testator, such as furniture, antiques, jewelry, and the like, to be distributed according to a written list which is not a part of the will. This permits change or additions to such gifts without the cost or formality required to amend the will. The will must make reference to such a list, and there are some basic rules which must be followed in making the list.

Usually the persons who are to receive the residue of the estate are the ones whom the testator is most interested in benefiting. A common danger in this type of will is that circumstances may change between the time the will is signed and the time the testator dies. As a result the will may do exactly the opposite of what the testator intended, and deny benefits to the very persons the will was intended to benefit. For example, assume father has an estate with a value of $1,000,000 at the time he prepares his will. He wants his spouse and children to receive the biggest part of his estate, but he also wants to remember a favorite charity. He provides for a charitable bequest of $100,000, with the rest of the estate (the residue) going to his spouse and children. However, the stock market declines and his estate shrinks to $500,000 by the time he dies. The charity still receives its $100,000, but the inheritance of the wife and family decline from $900,000 to $400.000. A result certainly not intended.

Consequently, when the father was thinking about making his charitable gift, he should have kept in mind that a decline in the value of his estate might unfairly impact the family. One way to prevent this is would have been to make the specific bequest in terms of fractional parts or percentages of the estate, rather than in terms of dollars and cents. If the father had given the charity 10% of his estate, rather than $100,000, the charity and the family would share proportionately in the decline of the value of the assets.

Provision for Alternate Disposition of the Property

When a testator provides that most of the property shall go to a certain person, it ordinarily is wise to also provide for a secondary beneficiary in the event that the first person dies before the testator. Many people want to make a chain of alternatives by providing the property shall go to "A, but if he is dead, then to Mrs. A, but if she is dead, then to B," and so on. While it is not practical to provide a long chain of alternative dispositions, it is advisable to have a final beneficiary that will certainly exist at the testator's death, whether a group of persons ("my heirs at law"), or an entity such as a charity.

Provision for Common Accident or Successive Deaths

It is not unusual for a husband and wife to be killed as the result of a common accident, or under circumstances that make it difficult to determine who died first. Because the husband's will usually provides for the wife to take some or all of his property, and vice versa, this type of accident can lead to serious problems.

Suppose a husband's will leaves all his property to his wife, with an alternate gift to his parents in the event that she dies before he does, and the wife has left all of her property to the husband, with an alternate gift to her parents. Then, in a common accident the husband dies first and the wife dies a week later. Immediately upon the husband's death, title to his property will go to his wife; and a week later, when the wife dies, title to the property will go to her parents, eliminating his family entirely. Such a double passage of title within a week could also result in the levying of federal estate taxes and require probate administration of the property twice.

Some lawyers use a clause requiring each beneficiary to survive by a specified period of time, such as 30 days, although delays are permitted up to 6 months under federal tax regulations.

The Colorado Probate Code requires a beneficiary to survive by 120 hours (5 days) in order to inherit property. This amendment can be overridden by a specific provision in a will.

Other problems can arise if a husband and wife have wills of this kind, and both die from the same accident, but it is not known with certainty who died first. The husband's parents may claim the property by asserting that the wife died first, with the wife's parents arguing the contrary. An expensive lawsuit may be required to settle the dispute. Also, when one of the spouses owns most or all of the couple's property, the order of death may be important in determining the tax consequences of the estate plan. A common provision in the wills is to create a presumption that the spouse with the greatest wealth survived the other spouse.

Powers for the Personal Representative

In order to administer the estate with the least amount of time, trouble, and expense, the personal representative should be given broad powers. Special wording should be used in the will to provide those powers. The Colorado Fiduciaries' Powers Act gives broad powers to the personal representative unless express limits are contained in the will. Those powers should be specifically enumerated and set out in the will so that there is no doubt that they will be available in a state other than Colorado where such powers are not granted by statute. Since the powers are usually quite broad, there may be situations where the testator wants restrictions placed on the personal representative.

Provision for Guardianship and Conservatorship

When the testator has minor children, the will should appoint a guardian for the children to serve if the other parent dies before the will takes effect, or if the other parent fails or ceases to serve as guardian for any reason (for example, if the other parent is incapacitated). The guardian is the person who assumes the parent's responsibility for the care and education of the minor child. The will can also appoint a conservator of the minor children's property. The conservator is the person having the responsibility for the care and management of the minor's assets. The guardian and the conservator need not be the same person. In some cases, it might be appropriate to have a friend or family member appointed as the guardian, and a bank or trust company appointed as the conservator. In Colorado, a child over 12 years of age may select his own guardian, subject to court approval. But for the guidance of the court, it may be wise to name a guardian in the will, even if the child is over 12.

Contingent Management Provision

A minor child does not have the legal capacity to manage property. The parent of a minor child cannot automatically manage the minor's property without court proceedings (typically a conservatorship for the property), which can be cumbersome and expensive. For this reason, provisions should be made in the will to avoid the need for creation of a conservatorship for any property passing under the will to a minor child. The will may create a trust for minor children, or may provide that property a minor child would otherwise take outright will pass to a custodian for the minor under the Colorado Uniform Transfers to Minors Act. The personal representative of the estate can then appoint the minor's guardian, or an adult member of the minor's family, to serve as the custodian to manage the minor's property until the minor reaches 18 years of age.

Required Formalities

A will must, of course, be signed by the testator. Unless the will is entirely written in the testator's own handwriting and signed by the testator (called a holographic will), the requirements of a valid will are: (1) it must be in writing, (2) signed by the testator, or by some other person on behalf of the testator in the "conscious" presence of the testator and at the testator's direction, and (3) signed by two witnesses either before or after the testator's death, each of whom, in the "conscious" presence of the testator, witnessed the signing, or witnessed the testator's acknowledgment of his signature, or witnessed the testator's acknowledgment that the writing was his will. "Conscious" presence means physical proximity to the testator, but not necessarily within the testator's line of sight. These are strict requirements designed to prevent fraud. If a document is not executed with the above formalities, it may, on rare occasions, still be admitted to probate as a will if it can be proven with clear and convincing evidence that the testator intended the document to be a will.

Although Colorado law does not prohibit a beneficiary from also being a witness to the will, it may avoid future conflicts if the witnesses are disinterested third parties. In the usual will, the signature of the testator is followed by a clause (called the "attestation clause") signed by the witnesses reciting that the statutory requirements have been satisfied.

"Self-Proving" Will

Colorado also allows for a will to be "self-proved" by an affidavit, signed by the testator and witnesses before a notary public. The cost and inconvenience of probating the will may be reduced if the testator and the witnesses make the will "self-proving." However, this formality is not required, and a will is perfectly valid even if it is not signed before a notary public, if it meets the statutory requirements.

Summary

In Colorado, a testator has an almost unlimited freedom in determining to whom, and how, the estate should be distributed at death. The will should be "tailor-made" to carry out the testator's wishes and meet the individual needs and circumstances of each estate. However, unless certain formalities are observed, and certain common problems are considered, the desires of the testator may be frustrated and the beneficiaries named in his will may get nothing, or may receive an estate greatly decreased by unnecessary and costly administrative expenses, death taxes, income taxes, and litigation.

PITFALLS OF A HOMEMADE WILL

A single conversation across the table with a wise man is worth a month's study of books.

— Chinese Proverb

Testators who decide to prepare their own wills probably think they are saving attorney fees. Lawyers know that testators who make their own wills often create disputes that only costly litigation can settle. Studying books available in the library and bookstore may give the layman a false sense of confidence in their ability to navigate the sometimes tricky waters of putting desires into the appropriate language. Since common everyday language may have special significance when used in a legal context like a will, testators are advised, at a minimum, to have an attorney review their wills for any potential legal pitfalls. The experience of a qualified estate-planning attorney may seem unnecessary, but the do-it-yourself estate planner may end up with a will something like that embodied in the following actual instrument:

Terrell Tex Jan 12-1950

this Letter is Written With the idea that Some thing might happen to me. that I would be wiped out Suddenly if this Should Happen my business would be in awful shape no relatives, nobody to do a thing So, this is written to have my affairs wound up in a reasonable way in case of my Sudden Death. Would Like to have all of my affairs, Cash all assets including any Bank Balance turned over to Parties named below With out any Bond or any Court action that can be avoided. they to wind up my affairs in any way they See fit.

U. C. Boyles Refrigeration Supply Co. Charlie Hill Superior Ice Co

Should these Gentleman need a third man Would Suggest Walker. National Bank of Commerce Each of these Gentleman to receive $500.000 for his Services

I have tried to make my wishes plain. of Course these Crooked Lawyers Would want a Lot of Whereas and Wherefores included in this. Not much in favor of the organized Charities they are too Cold blooded also not much in Favor of any person over 21-Benefitting by my Kick off unless there is a good reason am inclined to play the children they are not Responsible for being here and can't help themselves

Terrell-Feb. 7-1950

have Let this Letter get cold and Read it again-to See if it Seemed abut Right dont See much wrong except no whereas and Wherefores-excuse me

Lon Gresham

The testator would turn over in his grave if he knew that the instrument in which he had tried to make his "wishes plain" required two trips to the Supreme Court of Texas and excursions through several lower courts to fathom its meaning and consequences.

It is easy to laugh about some of the obvious problems in a will such as Gresham's, but many times learned people make errors just as costly when they draw their own will without legal counsel.

Is It a Valid Will?

One of the problems involved in the Gresham will was determining whether it was a will. If you read it carefully enough, you might begin to wonder if any property was actually disposed of and if it appointed personal representatives. The courts were divided on whether the instrument was a will. Ultimately the Supreme Court of Texas held that the instrument was a will which disposed of no property but appointed personal representatives to administer the estate.

Often testators leave letters (sometimes even on the back of a match folder) expressing a thought that something should be done upon their deaths. The courts may have difficulty deciding whether such a writing was intended to be the decedent's last will and testament, or was simply the expression of a wish or hope.

The Holographic Will

As discussed in Chapters 11 and 12, there are two kinds of wills which the layman may attempt to make for himself. One, a "holographic" will, is wholly in the maker's handwriting and is valid in Colorado (contrary to the law of some other states). The second is one that is typed or otherwise not wholly in the handwriting of the testator. Such an instrument must be executed in accordance with certain prescribed legal requirements or it is void. If a purported will is partly handwritten and partly typed, it is valid only if properly signed and witnessed.

Was It Properly Executed?

One of the dangers of a will written without professional advice is that the testator may not give sufficient attention to the legal requirements for a valid execution of a will. If these requirements are not followed, the writing cannot be admitted to probate as a will. The requirements for a valid will vary from state to state. Chapter 12 describes the execution requirements in Colorado.

Where Is the Will? Are the Witnesses Available?

One of the reasons for executing a will in a lawyer's office is that the witnesses may be more easily located if their testimony is required at the time the will is submitted for probate. The attorney may also retain a copy of the will in his office to evidence the contents of the original will itself as a safeguard should it be lost or destroyed. Family members should be advised of the existence of the will and its location.

Ambiguity

One of the great problems involved in a do-it-yourself will is ambiguity. The central question is: "What did the testator really intend?" Laypersons write in a manner which may be clear to them, but may be ambiguous to lawyers and judges. Here are some examples that could lead to costly litigation and end up actually frustrating the intent of the testator.

Everything to the Wife — What's Left to the Children

An expression which is sometimes found in a will written without legal advice is: "I give my wife everything I have, and upon her death I give what is left for the benefit of my children." Problems are created by such phrasing. Does the wife get the property, or only the right to use it for life? May she sell, mortgage, or lease the property, and if so, how may she invest the proceeds of sale? What happens if the wife mingles the husband's property with her own (including what she may acquire after his death)? Can she give the property away during her lifetime? Ordinarily, the words "for the benefit of" create a trust. Is a trust being created for the children? If a trust is created, who is the trustee, and what are the terms of the trust? When does the trust come to an end? These are merely some of the questions raised by such wording.

Gift of Money; Gift of Land

If a testator states, "I give $25,000 to my three sons," does he mean $25,000 to be divided among the three sons, or does he mean $25,000 to each? If he declares "I give all my land in Jefferson County to my son," and the land is subject to a mortgage, does the son have to pay the mortgage, or does the estate pay it?

Money on Deposit in Bank

Another type of ambiguity is that involved in a gift of money on deposit in a bank. Does the statement: "I leave the money on deposit at the Fourth National Bank" mean only what was on hand when the will was made (say $1,000), or does it mean the amount on hand when the decedent died (say $25,000). If it turns out that at the time of the testator's death there are two bank accounts, a checking account which existed when the will was made and a savings account was opened later, who gets what?

Gifts of Shares of Stock

Suppose a testator gives to a beneficiary $1,000 or 10 shares of XYZ stock (worth $100 per share at the time of the making of the will). What does the personal representative do if the XYZ stock is worth $500 a share ($5,000) at the testator's death? Does the beneficiary have his choice?

Another recurring problem is the gift of a specific number of shares of stock without reference to stock splits or stock dividends. For example, the testator may give 100 shares of XYZ stock, this being all of the shares owned at the time of the making of the will. Later, a stock dividend of 5 shares for each one of the original 100 shares is declared. If the provision is interpreted literally, the recipient of 100 shares may be entitled to only one-fifth the number of shares the testator may have intended.

Gift of a Business Interest

Consider the following statement: "I give my business to my son." What happens to the accounts receivables, the inventories, the cash in the bank, and other assets belonging to the business? What if the business is located on a piece of land owned by the testator; who gets the land?

Is It Tailored to the Testator's Needs?

One of the real advantages of obtaining professional advice about what to put in a will is that such discussion helps the testator decide what his basic desires are, what they wish to do with their property, and what alternatives are available to achieve these objectives. Thus, the testator will more carefully consider the nature and extent of all the assets, and the possible ways in which family, friends, business associates, and charitable interests can be assisted. The testator may be made aware of possibilities he never considered before.

For example, if a man merely wills his property to his wife or to his children, he may fail to provide properly for the continuation of a business, or the handling of a partnership interest, or in some other way handicap his surviving business associates. All of these things can be specifically handled in the will, or otherwise during his lifetime, in a way that combines the greatest amount of benefit for his family with the least amount of disruption by his death. Often such matters are overlooked by a person making his own will, or complicated by incomplete or ambiguous dispositions.

Does It Unintentionally Disinherit Family Members and Others?

If a testator prepares the testator's own will, the testator may fail to provide for certain persons who are intended to be the beneficiaries. For example, a person may leave property to an only son, or, if the son is not living at the testator's death, to the son's children. If the son does not in fact survive the testator, the daughter-in-law will get nothing. However, she must raise the minor children, who will get all the entire inheritance, and she will likely be required to do so under the restrictions of a court-supervised conservatorship, which will continue until the children become 18 years old. Such a conservatorship would require the added expense of applications to and orders from the court to do various things in connection with the estate. It would further require the filing of reports, and the filing and court approval of accountings, including a final accounting when each child reaches age 18.

Children of a prior marriage may be disinherited inadvertently. An outright gift to a surviving spouse, followed by the death of that spouse, could result in the surviving spouse's children getting the entire inheritance, leaving the children of the prior marriage with nothing.

Sometimes a testator writing his own will makes large bequests of money to friends or others. Such incidental bequests may leave little for the primary beneficiaries due to shrinkage in the estate, or because of a failure to account for estate liabilities.

Other Significant Omissions

Many other important matters are often overlooked in the self-made will. There may be a failure to give directions regarding payment of taxes due as a result of proceeds of a life insurance policy. The estate without the insurance may be non-taxable, but the large insurance policy could cause the estate to have to pay an estate tax. Who should pay the tax on the insurance proceeds — the individual named in the policy to receive the death benefit, or the persons entitled to the residue of the estate under the will?

The self-made will may fail to designate a successor personal representative or trustee in the event the original named personal representative or trustee fails to serve or dies. In the absence of the designation of a successor, the administration would have to proceed with a personal representative or trustee appointed by the court.

Sufficient attention may not be given to the possibility of one death occurring within a short time of another. If a decedent gives all property to a surviving spouse, and if the spouse then dies within a short period of time without having a will, all the decedent's property may go to the surviving spouse's family, to the complete exclusion of decedent's family.

Summary

There are many reasons why it is not advisable for a person inexperienced in legal terms and consequences to attempt to execute his own will. Such wills constitute a prolific source of litigation, with resulting family disputes and greatly increased costs of probate.

This poem by Lord Neaves is dedicated to those seeking to avoid the lawyers' fee for preparing a will:

> *Ye lawyers who live upon litigants' fees,*
> *And who need a good many to live at your ease,*
> *Grave or gay, wise or witty, whate'er you decree,*
> *Plain stuff or Queen's Counsel, take counsel of me.*
> *When a festive occasion your spirit unbends,*
> *You should never forget the Profession's best friends;*
> *So we'll send round the wine and bright bumper fill,*
> *To the jolly testator who makes his own will.*

14

CHOOSING THE RIGHT PERSONAL REPRESENTATIVE

Any damned fool can write a plan. It's the execution
that gets you all screwed up.
— James F. Hollingsworth

Under prior law, an executor was the person named in the will and appointed by the court to administer the affairs of a decedent's estate. Where there was no will, or where the will failed to name a person who was able and willing to manage the estate, the one appointed by the court for this task was formerly called an administrator. With the enactment of the Colorado Probate Code in 1974, the terms "executor" and "administrator" were replaced with the single term "personal representative."

Selecting the right personal representative is one of the testator's most important decisions. The one appointed will be your agent to carry out the wishes and desires expressed in your will. Integrity, business experience, impartiality, willingness to serve, and sound judgment should be taken into consideration when selecting a personal representative.

Duties and Powers

The personal representative's goal is to handle the estate in the very best interests of the persons who will inherit it. The personal representative should preserve and manage the estate, and see to the payment of obligations. The assets of the estate should be treated fairly, impartially, and confidentially.

The powers given to a personal representative in a will may be limited to paying debts, expenses, and taxes. The powers also may be broad, and include the right to dispose of property, make divisions among the beneficiaries, and operate a business.

Certain actions are necessary in any estate where there is a will naming a personal representative. Within a reasonable time after the testator's death, the original will should be taken to the attorney representing the personal representative, who will lodge the will with the appropriate court and file a petition for its probate. At that time, the personal representative should generally know the nature and extent of the properties of the estate. After the petition is filed and proper notice is given, a court hearing is held in order to prove the will and admit it to probate. However, if the will is a "self-proving" will, as discussed elsewhere in this book, it may be admitted to probate without a hearing. The personal representative then qualifies (typically by filing an acceptance of appointment) and secures authority from the court to act, issued in the form of letters.

The personal representative is responsible for ascertaining the properties owned by the testator, as well as the outstanding debts and obligations. The personal representative must prepare an inventory of the properties to be submitted to the court or the beneficiaries of the estate. If there is an on-going business, the personal representative must supervise it. It is most important that the proper insurance be kept in force on the properties, and that any rights the estate might have be kept intact. After debts have been paid, including whatever taxes are due, the personal representative gives a final accounting, and makes distributions to the beneficiaries as directed under the will. For more information on the personal representative's duties, see Chapters 1 and 5.

Whom Should I Choose as Personal Representative?

The Surviving Spouse

The surviving spouse may be capable of assuming the responsibilities of the estate. Frequently, however, the spouse is untrained in the business of probate and tax problems. Under such circumstances, it may be better to appoint a bank, a trust company, a partner, another member of the family, or a trusted friend as personal representative. Eventually, the surviving spouse will be expected to manage his own affairs, but this can be done gradually as some knowledge of the problems involved is acquired. Perhaps a co-personal representative is the answer. The surviving spouse can act together with the steadying hand of one more experienced.

Banks or Trust Companies

Certain banks and trust companies have been granted trust powers by the state banking commission. State and federal authorities strictly supervise their trust departments. Many banks and trust companies, through decades of experience, have evolved systems and procedures that will protect the estate while relieving the surviving spouse of the myriad of details that would otherwise have been his responsibility as personal representative. Banks and trust companies may also provide the ideal neutral party if a family dispute were to arise. Their institutional nature insures longevity. As personal representative, a bank or trust company may employ the testator's own attorney and accountant in handling the estate. Instructions may be left either in the will, or separately, which may recommend an attorney and accountant. Alternatively, rather than naming a corporate fiduciary, an individual personal representative may be named and that person may selectively employ certain banks or trust companies to perform specific tasks to ease the administration of an estate.

Compensation of a Personal Representative

The personal representative is entitled to a "reasonable fee" under Colorado law. This fee is determined according to such factors as the experience of the person, the complexity of the estate, and any other pertinent considerations. (See Chapter 2 for additional information regarding reasonable compensation).

The law in Colorado prior to 1974 (and the law in many states today) provided that the personal representative was entitled to receive a commission computed at statutory rates based on the value of the assets of the estate, which covered all ordinary services of the personal representative. If extraordinary services were required, the court could have allowed the personal representative additional compensation.

An individual, whether it is the surviving spouse, a child, or a trusted friend, although entitled to charge the same fee as any other personal representative, may, for personal reasons, charge little, if anything, other than actual expenses incurred. If the personal representative does not intend to collect a fee, a written waiver should be signed and filed with the court; otherwise, the IRS may take the position that the personal representative is taxed on the amount allowed under the statute, even if the fee is not paid. This is due to a tax doctrine known as "constructive receipt."

An Alternate Personal Representative

A personal representative must, of course, live longer than the person making the appointment. It may be well, therefore, not to name someone more advanced in age than the testator. The vicissitudes of life are such that an alternate or successor personal representative should be named in every will, with the same powers and rights as the first personal representative named.

It is legal, though not wise, to attempt to draw one's own will. There are numerous pitfalls which may make that attempt to save money a most expensive mistake (See Chapter 13 for further discussion regarding the potential problems with homemade wills).

This includes naming a personal representative without the proper expressions concerning powers and responsibilities.

Powers of a Personal Representative

The Colorado Probate Code covers the powers and responsibilities of personal representatives. The Colorado Fiduciaries' Powers Act grants extensive powers in administering the estate. This avoids the need for frequent recourse to the court for instructions. Provisions in the will may broaden the statutory powers. The will can grant the personal representative specially drafted powers to sell and lease property of the estate, to continue a business owned by the decedent, and to invest surplus funds of the estate in a specified manner. The will can also authorize the personal representative to serve without bond. Unless bond is waived in the will or by all of the beneficiaries, the personal representative (except a bank or trust company) may be required to be bonded at additional expense to the estate.

Co-Personal Representatives

Naming two or more persons as co-personal representatives may solve the problem of choosing the right personal representative. You may not want to name one child over another for fear of the possible friction. This problem may be solved by naming two or more children as co-personal representatives, or merely by naming a neutral personal representative.

It is common for a husband or wife to name the survivor as personal representative. The surviving spouse may be entirely capable of being personal representative, and, as such, would act with the utmost in economy to the estate. However, a surviving spouse is often at a complete loss when the complex problems of modern business are suddenly thrust upon him. Under such circumstances, the surviving spouse might welcome the services of a friend, or the trust department of a bank or trust company, as co-personal representative. When a bank or trust company acts as co-personal representative, it usually maintains physical custody of bonds, securities, and other properties of the estate, subject, of course, to the right of the co-personal representative to inspect the properties and records during business hours.

Other than to pay funeral charges and take necessary measures for preservation of the estate, a personal representative cannot act until the will is admitted to probate by the court, and he is appointed and qualified. There may, however, be certain urgent matters which require attention before the personal representative can formally qualify. If the decedent was engaged in an on-going business, it should continue to operate. If there are perishable assets in the estate, they should be protected. It may be necessary to arrange for funds to take care of expenses incidental to the operation of an on-going business, or from the decedent's last illness. In choosing a personal representative the testator should consider the willingness and ability of the person or institution named to take immediate action. This includes petitioning the court for appointment as special administrator of the estate, requesting the court authorize the person to take prescribed actions as are required to preserve the estate assets — pending admission of the will to probate, and the appointment of the personal representative.

Telling Your Personal Representative Your Intentions

Before being named in a will, the designated personal representative should be consulted to determine whether he is willing to act. The proposed personal representative may be unwilling or unable to assume the responsibility. The testator then can ascertain the reason and accommodate the concerns, or select someone else. If the will provides for the personal representative to exercise discretion to resolve conflicts between the beneficiaries, the testator should discuss his expectations so the personal representative will have had the benefit of personal guidance in what could be a difficult situation. Moreover, the testator may wish to organize all of his papers in one location so that the personal representative does not have to hunt for them and run the risk of mishandling an asset, or worse yet missing an asset altogether. Some find a simple accordion file with a separate slot devoted to each asset very helpful. After the will is prepared, it is a good practice to furnish the personal representative with a copy of the will, or to inform the personal representative where the original will has been located for safekeeping.

Attributes of a Personal Representative

Considerations in choosing the personal representative are much the same as those for choosing a business partner. The necessary attributes may be summarized as follows:

- *Integrity.* A personal representative should have the ultimate interests of the heirs in mind at all times. This requires soundness of moral principle and character. The person must be unselfish and honest in the handling of the estate.
- *Business ability.* Sound business judgment, combined with actual experience, is a desired quality. Many economies result from experience, and the testator's ultimate aim is to see that as much of the estate as possible passes to the beneficiaries.
- *Experience.* The handling of an estate requires knowledge of the rights and responsibilities of a personal representative, and the ability to carry them out. With larger estates, knowledge of both income and estate taxation is necessary.
- *Availability.* The time a personal representative must devote to the handling of the estate depends on its size and complexity. If a personal representative is to keep the best interests of the beneficiaries in mind, there must be availability of time to devote to the estate. In handling large estates, the duties may be so time consuming that an individual personal representative would have to neglect personal business interests. In such a case, a trust institution should be considered, since it has available officers and employees specially trained in handling estate matters.

- *Impartiality.* Whether the personal representative is the surviving spouse, child, friend, or a trust institution, complete impartiality must be given to all heirs under the will. Such impartiality may be impossible from a member of the family. If the testator believes this to be the case, he should consider naming someone outside of the family.

- *Discretion.* Handling an estate may bring a personal representative into contact with family problems which neither the testator, nor surviving family members, wants publicly aired. It is therefore important that the personal representative be a person who will conduct estate matters confidentially. It is a privilege to serve the testator, and it is the testator's right to expect matters that were held in confidence during his lifetime will be so maintained after death.

Summary

The testator intends for the accumulation of a lifetime to be handled prudently. Therefore, a personal representative should be selected who possesses sound business judgment tempered with concern for the beneficiaries.

In recent years, people have given more thought to planning their estates than in the past. This is attributable to the ever-growing difficulty of accumulating, managing, and preserving property. Taxation and its adverse effects are of special concern. A will, no matter how simple, should be prepared for every property owner. Preparation of the will should include earnest attention to the selection of a personal representative. A personal representative, in order to serve the estate in the best possible way, must, like the operator of a successful business, have the necessary experience, knowledge, and seasoned judgment, as well as the time to devote to estate affairs.

JOINTLY OWNED PROPERTY

Origin

Many people believe that an ideal method of owning property is "joint tenancy with right of survivorship." Although there are advantages of joint ownership of property, there are several disadvantages which should be carefully considered. Even with the now widespread use of joint tenancies for certificates of deposit and other cash-equivalent investments, the ownership of property with right of survivorship is not a new idea. It was an early common law favorite. If two or more persons bought property and took title in both names, the presumption was that they intended to own it with right of survivorship. So, if land was sold to John Doe and John Smith, upon the death of either owner, the surviving owner automatically received the interest of the deceased owner and had title to the entire property. The reasoning was that when one owner died, the person's interest in the property also died, and the survivor owned all. This was their agreement.

From a practical standpoint, the chief characteristic of joint tenancy is that the survivor owns the entire interest. The appealing aspect of joint tenancy ownership is the saving of time and expense in probate by permitting the survivor to own the property automatically. Under the early common law in England, the purpose of joint tenancy was to minimize or avoid feudal tenures or duties, the predecessors of present day death taxes.

In time, this chief characteristic lost its appeal, partly because of the abolition of the early feudal taxes, and partly because it became less desirable to have the ultimate ownership dependent on the chance of survival. The owner of a joint interest could not dispose of it by a will. If a joint owner died without a will, that deceased owner's interest would not go to his heirs. If a joint tenant wanted the interest to go at death to somebody other than the surviving joint tenant, the joint tenancy had to be severed while both of the joint tenants were living.

Tenancy in Common

The presumption of feudal times changed during subsequent common law development from that favoring right of survivorship, to that favoring a tenancy in common ownership. Under this presumption, if two persons bought land together, it was presumed that they owned it as tenants in common. Unlike the joint tenancy earlier favored, if either joint owner died, his interest would pass under his will, and if he died without a will, his interest would pass to his heirs. Therefore, at either owner's death, the survivor would not own any greater interest than was owned before the death of the co-tenant. The chief characteristic of tenancy in common, then, is that the deceased co-tenant's interest passes as a part of the co-tenant's estate, instead of automatically passing to the surviving co-tenant by reason of survivorship.

All states now have express statutes concerning these early presumptions. These statutes generally provide that if parties buy property and take title in both names, it shall not be presumed that they own it with right of survivorship, but as tenants in common. In Colorado, as in most states, the joint tenancy right of survivorship is possible, but it must be clearly shown that this was the intention of the owners.

Creating Joint Tenancy

Colorado statutes make specific provision for the creation of joint tenancy with respect to both real estate and personal property. The statutes provide that joint tenancy is created in the instrument conveying title to the property only if it is declared that the property is conveyed in joint tenancy. The classic language that is ordinarily used provides that title is being conveyed to the parties "as joint tenants with rights of survivorship and not as tenants in common." However, in Colorado, it is sufficient to simply convey the property to the parties "in joint tenancy," or as "joint tenants." Upon the death of either joint tenant, the recording of a certified copy of the death certificate serves to establish the surviving joint tenant's complete ownership.

Government Bonds

Frequently U.S. Bonds are registered in two or more names. A common method of registering such bonds is "John Doe or Mary Doe (husband and wife)." Such bonds typically do not contain the designation of the owners as "joint tenants" as required by the Colorado statute. If John or Mary Doe dies, does half the interest in these bonds pass under the decedent's will or does it belong to the survivor named on the bond? After conflicting court rulings in several states, it was held by the U.S. Supreme Court in 1962 that the survivor named on the bond became the sole owner at the death of the other co-owner. In this test case, a husband and wife in Texas had purchased bonds with community property funds. The bonds were valued at $87,035.50 when the wife died. In her will, she gave her share of the community property to her son. In a suit between the husband and the son to determine whether the mother's will was effective, the U.S. Supreme Court held that the bonds belonged solely to the surviving husband. The high court held that a Treasury Regulation which provided that the survivor became the sole owner upon the death of a co-owner was paramount to, and overruled any state law to the contrary. The Texas Supreme Court decision, which had given the surviving son half of the value of the bonds, was reversed.

When a U.S. Savings Bond is registered in the name of two individuals as co-owners, either may redeem it without permission of the other. Upon the death of one, the surviving co-owner becomes the sole owner. In that case, the bonds are not a part of the probate estate of the first to die, and are not liable for payment of the decedent's debts. Similarly, if a bond is registered, "Richard Brown, payable on death to Richard Brown, Jr.," then upon the death of Richard Brown, the named beneficiary becomes the sole owner, and the bond is not part of the probate estate of the original owner, or subject to the original owner's debts.

Bank Accounts

Many people fail to distinguish and understand the difference between an agency account and a survivorship account. "Joint account" is the popular term, but is misleading. The terms "convenience account" (also called "agency account" or "authorization account") and "survivorship account" should be used to distinguish clearly between the two different type accounts in a bank or savings and loan association which are held in the name of two or more persons.

A lack of understanding of the consequences of survivorship provisions often causes unintended results with joint accounts. Competent legal advice should be sought before creating joint accounts of significant size in which the joint party may not be the sole intended beneficiary of the owner's estate.

A typical person likely to have a bank account on which two or more people are authorized to sign checks is the elderly widow who lives alone. The widow generally wants someone to be authorized to sign checks to pay her bills. Therefore, she authorizes someone else — a child, a bookkeeper, a nurse, or the next-door-neighbor — to sign checks on her account. The question that must be determined is whether the widow owning the account wants the co-signer to eventually own the balance of the account. If so, she asks for a signature card, signed by both the widow and the co-signer, which contains the express provision "as joint tenants with right of survivorship and not as tenants in common." This clearly indicates that the elderly widow wants the co-signer to have the funds in her account at her death. This is a simple substitute for a provision in her will.

However, if the widow wants the co-signer to sign checks only as her agent, she asks for an "authorization," or "agency," or "power of attorney" card. The widow uses this method when there is no intent to pass ownership of the balance of the account to the co-signer. The balance is to become a part of the widow's estate at her death. The point is that there is nothing objectionable to the widow's giving the balance to the friend or relative who is assisting her in her business matters, but the problem comes after the widow's death, when the question arises: "Did the widow intend that this friend or relative own what was left in the bank?"

Effect of Joint Ownership on Taxes

There are no estate tax advantages in owning property in joint tenancy, but there can be tax disadvantages. Many people believe that by placing property in a survivorship form, it will not be subject to a death tax. This is not so. Any assets shown to be owned by a decedent, whether placed in joint tenancy or not, will be subject to estate tax if the value of all assets in an estate exceeds the value of assets sheltered by the federal estate and gift tax exemption. This credit will allow tax-free passage of substantial amounts of property. The unlimited marital deduction provisions of the federal estate and gift tax statutes now allow tax-free passage of unlimited amounts of property between spouses. Parties with substantial estates, including jointly owned property, should obtain the advice of an attorney knowledgeable in estate planning before making major plans or changes in the ownership of property, or its potential distribution at death.

Summary

Joint ownership of property can reduce the original owner's complete control over the property. Sharing ownership also results in sharing management and control of the property with the joint owner. This may not be a problem if the owners are harmonious, but the family picture can change through a divorce or family squabble.

The owner of joint property should keep in mind three areas in which problems have arisen: (1) subsequent ownership and management of the property prior to the death of first joint owner to die, (2) liability of jointly owned property for debts of either named co-owner, and (3) taxation by both state and federal governments on jointly owned property. The owner of a bank account should clearly understand the distinction between a "convenience of authorization (agency)" and a "joint tenancy with right of survivorship" account. In the former, the authorized person or agent does not acquire ownership of the balance in the bank account at the death of the owner; in the latter, the survivor does acquire ownership in the balance.

Often, the advantages of passing ownership to the survivor are outweighed by incurring death tax disadvantages, or having the ultimate ownership in a person other than the original owner of the property desired. A change in joint ownership, or in ultimate disposition of jointly held property, cannot be changed by a will. Before placing property in survivorship form, the owner should clearly understand the effect of sharing ownership of property with another prior to the original owner's death.

WHAT IS COMMUNITY PROPERTY?

Colorado does not have the form of property ownership known as "community property." We are what is called a "common law" state. However, because of our proximity to those states that are community property states, and due to the mobility that exists today, many persons living in Colorado may have transported community property with them when moving here. Colorado does recognize the existence, and the legal consequences, of community property where its origin can be effectively traced.

The community property system is primarily derived from Spanish-Mexican law. The system is based on a theory that a husband and wife form a "community" and that property acquired during the existence of the marriage belongs equally to both spouses. Although some of the fifty states have adopted certain aspects of community property law, only eight states currently have a fully developed community property system. These states are Louisiana, Texas, New Mexico, Arizona, Nevada, California, Washington, and Idaho. Wisconsin and Alaska also have a variation of community property. Although a common basis underlies the community property systems of these eight states, important differences exist from one state to another. Each of these community property systems is unique in many ways.

Definition of Community Property

To determine what community property is, it is first necessary to consider what it is not. Property owned by a husband or wife before marriage is that person's "separate property." Property received after marriage by gift or inheritance is also the separate property of the person receiving it, as is a judgment for pain and suffering following an injury to either spouse. "Community property" is what is left. That is, community property is all property acquired by either spouse during marriage which is not separate property.

In case of doubt about the nature of a particular asset, those states having community property will presume everything owned by a married couple to be community property, and it will be so judged in the absence of evidence establishing it as separate. The legal principles are simple enough, but their application can be extremely difficult, partly because the question of what is separate and what is community usually does not arise until the marriage is terminated by death or divorce. In the first case, one of the persons knowing essential facts is dead. In the second, the evidence of how and when certain assets were acquired may be tinged with bitterness and be unreliable.

Community property is not affected by the name in which the property is titled. Assets may be titled in the sole name of either spouse, but that does not change the fact that both spouses are treated as owning one-half of the property. If community property is titled in the name of only one spouse, that spouse is treated as being the manager or custodian of the other spouse's interest in the property. For this reason, in community property states, the signatures of both spouses are required to transfer an asset.

Record Keeping and Tracing

If the husband and wife have the foresight and the financial means to establish and maintain a reliable set of records, carefully segregating separate assets and channeling all cash receipts in the proper manner, there is little difficulty in determining the character of their assets when the marriage is dissolved. On the other hand, if records are poorly kept, or if cash revenues have been indiscriminately mingled without regard to their source, the determination can become difficult, even impossible. Courts will make every effort to trace a questionable asset to its source, but if there is no evidence that the asset is the separate property of either spouse, it will be presumed to be community and so treated by the court. Tracing assets has long been a popular activity for accountants, lawyers, and judges confronted with questions of this kind.

Revenues from Separate Property

A large part of the trouble in distinguishing separate property from community property results from the assumption, by many couples, that while living in a community property state, revenue from a separate asset is itself separate. Unfortunately, in some community property states, the opposite is true, unless the husband and wife have entered into the kind of agreement described in the following paragraph. Some courts have long held that income from a separate asset is to be treated as community property. This includes rent from separate real estate; delay rentals from an oil and gas lease covering separately owned real estate; salaries, wages, and other earnings of both husband and wife; interest and cash dividends on separately owned securities; and, profits from the sale of separately owned livestock. Without a written agreement, the only kinds of revenues sometimes considered to be the separate property of the spouse who owns the asset from which such revenues are derived, are those which represent the return of capital, such as oil and gas royalties, a bonus received for making the lease, and stock dividends and splits. A profit from the sale of a separately owned asset is usually treated as the separate property of the spouse concerned.

Agreements Terminating or Creating Community Property

Some community property states provide that a husband and wife can voluntarily partition, or separate, all or part of their community into separate property. A written instrument, signed by both parties, is all that may be required. Such a partition is probably not valid as to creditors or good faith purchasers without notice, until the instrument is placed of record in the county where any real property is situated. Some states even permit an oral partition.

Community property may also be converted to separate property through a gift of such property from one spouse to the other as long as the requisite donative intent exists, and the gift is not made so as to defraud or injure creditors or other third parties.

Community property law contains no provision for converting separate property to community property by a deed or other voluntary act of the parties. An attempt to do so would probably result in a tenancy in common. However, a "scrambling" of separate and community funds, if carried on long enough, would probably result in an eventual loss of the proof that an asset was originally separate and, as noted above, in the absence of such proof, the asset will be presumed to be community.

The community estate of new community property state residents begins when their first earnings, or other community receipts, reach their hands. There is no automatic conversion into community property of assets previously acquired; real estate (land and buildings) in a separate property state where the couple formerly lived, as well as personal property brought into the community property state, will remain the separate property of the owners if it was separate when acquired. But such an asset may lose its separate character through changes in form or from mingling community receipts with the separate asset.

Married persons who leave a community property state do not thereby automatically convert their community property to separate property. Real estate, if it is community property at the time of the owners' move will remain so, and the determination whether it is community or separate is usually a question of the law of the state where it is located. Even a Colorado court would apply the law of the state in which the land is located. Property other than land follows the owner and loses some of its community attributes when the owners move to a non-community property state and become subject to the laws of their new residence.

Either spouse can dispose of all their property, separate or community, by a valid will. Indeed, if the community property is titled in the sole name of a deceased spouse, it is not uncommon for the deceased spouse to provide in a will for the disposition of all the community property, both the deceased spouse's interest and the surviving spouse's interest. But the survivor is not bound to acquiesce in such an arrangement, and may elect to take his community interest in lieu of taking under the will. Although this is sometimes referred to as "the widow's election," it is also available to surviving husbands.

Management of the Community

For centuries, most community property states provided that the husband was the exclusive manager of the community, including that portion derived from the wife's separate estate or from her personal earnings. Most states have virtually eliminated the husband's exclusive management, and placed the wife on an equal footing. One spouse cannot make a gift of community personal property without the other's consent, nor may one spouse sell, encumber, or convey the community household furniture, furnishings, or the clothing of the other without the other's written consent. Certain restrictions also are imposed with respect to the transfer, lease, or mortgage of community real property.

Summary

The community property system represents an equitable method of permitting the wife, as well as the husband, to participate in the fruits and profits to be derived from their joint efforts. All property acquired during marriage is presumed to be community property, and will be treated so unless it can be shown to have its source in property owned before marriage, or received later by gift or inheritance. Those having separate property and wishing to preserve its identity can do so by the maintenance of orderly records which carefully distinguish between separate principal and community income. Those persons who may wish to convert their community interests to separate estates may do so by signing a partition agreement. Some community property states also allow separate property to be converted into community property by agreement.

THE REVOCABLE TRUST

The revocable trust, as an instrument in estate planning, has been increasingly popular in the past few years. A trust is the separation of the ownership of property into two parts with legal title (or management) of the property in one person, and beneficial ownership of the property in another person. There are two broad categories of trusts: the living trust and the testamentary trust. A living trust is created during the maker's lifetime, while a testamentary trust is created upon the maker's death by his will.

Further, there are two classes of living trusts, revocable and irrevocable. A revocable trust, as its name implies, is one that can be canceled, or changed, during its existence. Withdrawal of all or any part of the trust assets can be made at any time at the request of the maker of the revocable trust. An irrevocable trust, then, is one which cannot be altered. Irrevocable trusts are discussed further in Chapter 18.

It is also helpful to know the terms used in connection with trusts. The maker of a trust is the grantor or settlor. The person or bank who is given legal title, possession, and management of the trust assets, is the trustee. The person who is entitled to the income and other benefits from the trust is the beneficiary.

In creating the trust, the settlor desires to provide financial benefits to the beneficiary. However, rather than transferring the trust property directly to the beneficiary, the title is transferred to the trustee to hold and manage for the beneficiary. The reasons for this arrangement are discussed in the following sections.

Terms of a Typical Revocable Living Trust

In the typical revocable living trust, a grantor transfers property to a trustee under a written agreement. The agreement usually provides for the trustee to pay the grantor all of the income from the trust during his lifetime, together with such amounts of principal as may be requested by the grantor. It also provides that the grantor can amend or revoke the trust, or change the trustee at any time.

Upon the death of the grantor, the trust becomes irrevocable, meaning that the terms of the trust cannot thereafter be changed. The trust property is held, administered, and distributed as if it had passed under the grantor's will through probate, and into a testamentary trust. The provisions of the trust agreement which apply to the administration and distribution of the trust assets after the death of the grantor become operative upon the grantor's death, and are carried out immediately. There are no probate delays, and the publicity, normally necessary to probate a will is dispensed with.

A revocable living trust has a number of advantages, and only a few minor disadvantages, when compared with a testamentary trust. Illustration 17-1 shows the various aspects of a typical revocable living trust.

Illustration 17-1

The Revocable Living Trust

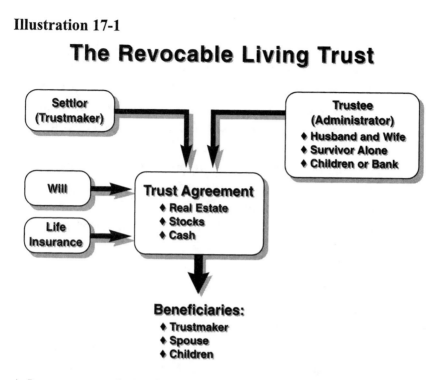

Advantages of the Revocable Living Trust

Management Uninterrupted by Incapacity

If a bank, or an experienced person, is selected as trustee of a revocable living trust, and a large part, or all, of the grantor's assets are placed in the trust during his lifetime, the revocable living trust can afford continuous experienced management of the trust assets regardless of the grantor's physical or mental incapacity. This avoids the necessity for a court declaration of incompetence, and the management of the assets by a court-appointed conservator. If the grantor of the trust desires to retain investment control of the trust assets, the trust agreement can provide that while the grantor is alive, and remains competent, no purchases or sales of the trust assets, or any other important actions can be made without his approval. Should the grantor become unable to manage his assets, either through mental or physical disabilities, the revocable living trust is the ideal instrument for continuing proper management.

In contrast, a power of attorney given to another person to manage the grantor's affairs will be automatically revoked upon the grantor's mental incapacity, unless the power of attorney is a "durable power of attorney" as described in Chapter 20. Also, the power of attorney will be automatically revoked upon the appointment, and qualification, of a conservator. Proceedings for the appointment of a conservator for the property of a person upon his becoming senile or incompetent, or upon his drifting in and out of lucid mental periods, can provoke unpleasant family quarrels. It certainly will involve court control of the assets of the incompetent, large legal and bonding fees, severe restrictions on investments, and much red tape.

The revocable living trust is the answer to these problems. The trustee can perform all of the necessary management of the trust assets, including the collection of income, the purchase and sale of trust assets, and the management of a closely held business or real estate. In addition the trustee can make payment of hospital, nursing and doctor bills, and other expenses of the grantor. When the period of temporary crisis ends, the grantor can revoke the trust if he so desires, or the grantor may again take up active management of his trust assets, while leaving the assets with the trustee. If the grantor dies, the trust can act as the grantor's will insofar as the assets of the trust are concerned.

Management for the Busy Executive or Professional

A revocable living trust is a valuable aid to the busy executive, or professional person, who does not have time to study the stock market or to do the many other things that are involved in managing the investment of valuable trust assets. A bank or other experienced trustee can supply experienced investment guidance and free a busy executive, or professional person, from worries that might interfere with the pursuit of the business or profession, while at the same time assuring continuous expert investment management of the trust assets.

Segregation of Assets

A revocable living trust also has the advantage of preventing certain properties from becoming mingled with other property. For example, if a wife has inherited property from her parents, and she desires that the property be kept separate from her husband's property, she can place her separate property with a bank in a revocable living trust. The trustee can maintain adequate records to keep that property segregated from the husband's assets.

Training the Trustee

The revocable living trust allows the grantor to observe the operation of the bank, or the family member, who will manage the estate at death. The trust maker can then be satisfied as to the manner in which assets will be managed and administered after death. Where a professional is to serve as trustee for the surviving spouse, this will also allow the surviving spouse to become familiar with the trust officer and lawyer, so that old friends, instead of strangers, will be there to take care of the spouse at death. If the surviving spouse is to become the successor trustee upon the grantor's death, the spouse will be able to become familiar with the operation of the trust, while the grantor is available to assist.

Privacy of Disposition of Assets at Death

Another advantage of the revocable living trust is the privacy afforded the grantor for the disposition of his estate at his death. Assets placed in a revocable living trust do not become a matter of public court record, as is the case with a probated will. Newspaper publicity about the grantor's assets and beneficiaries, and the plan for the disposition of the estate are thus avoided.

Reduction of Probate Expense

A revocable living trust may result in the reduction of probate expenses. Personal representative's commissions, attorney's fees, accounting fees, appraiser's fees, and other charges arising from the administration of a deceased person's estate are required by statute to be reasonable, but to a certain extent are based on the value of the assets passing under the decedent's will. (See Chapter 2 for further discussion regarding reasonable fees). Keeping property out of the probate or testamentary estate of the grantor can reduce such charges. If all of a grantor's assets are in a revocable living trust at the time of his death, it may not be necessary to go through probate at all. However, if a bank or non-family member is the initial trustee, this reduction may be offset, to some degree, by the trustee's cost to administer the trust assets during the grantor's lifetime. When the grantor owns property in more than one state, the avoidance of multiple probates can save substantial fees that would be duplicated in each state where property is located.

Avoidance of Will Contest

A revocable living trust is less vulnerable to attack by disgruntled heirs than is a will. It is rather easy for a relative to attack the probate of a will, even when the attack is based on flimsy reasons. It is quite expensive and time consuming for the personal representative to win a total victory in such a contest.

An attack can be made on a revocable living trust on the same grounds used to contest a will (lack of capacity or undue influence). However, such a contest does not tie up the trust assets in the same manner as a will contest ties up the probate assets. The burden of proof seems to lie more heavily with the trust contester, as the attacks are more often successful with wills, than with living trusts. The reason for this is that a will is merely a piece of paper until the testator's death. Nothing in a will has any effect or substance until after the will has been admitted to probate by a formal court order, and all assets are tied up until the will is settled. By contrast, a trust is in full force and effect at the moment of death of the grantor (because it was created during the grantor's life), and if there is a contest of the trust, the trustee has assets in his hands with which to pay for a defense of the trust.

Uninterrupted Management at Death

A revocable living trust provides a means for avoiding any interruption in the management of the trust's assets upon the grantor's death. Stocks, securities, real estate, and so on can continue to be managed, and debts, expenses of last illness, funeral bills, taxes, and so on can be paid without interruption. Further, there is no delay incurred in providing for the grantor's family immediately after his death. This elimination of delay is important when the trust property consists of assets which require day-to-day handling to avoid loss, and when the family has immediate financial requirements upon the death of the grantor.

Avoidance of Probate in Other States

If the grantor owns property physically located in different states, it may be possible to avoid expensive and time-consuming probate proceedings in these states by conveying the property to a trustee during the grantor's lifetime. However, if real estate in other states is to be placed in a revocable living trust, it is important to make sure that the laws of the state where the property is located allow a trustee from another state to act within that state, and that the laws in those states are followed when transferring property to the trust.

Tax Treatment of the Revocable Living Trust

Assets in a revocable living trust are taxable under the federal income tax, estate, and gift tax laws, and the Colorado estate tax laws, in the same manner as property owned outright by the grantor. No gift tax is payable when a grantor creates a revocable living trust. During the grantor's lifetime, all of the income of the trust is taxed to the grantor, and upon the grantor's death, all of the property in the revocable living trust is included in the grantor's estate for federal estate tax purposes. After the grantor's death, the trust becomes irrevocable, and the same tax advantages available to a testamentary trust are available to the living trust. These include the use of the unlimited marital deduction, or the avoidance of a second federal estate tax upon the spouse's estate, and the advantage of providing several different tax entities for federal income tax purposes.

Summary

By using a revocable living trust, a person may select a trustee to manage assets in the event he should become incapacitated, rather than having a person appointed by the court manage his assets. While competent, the grantor can continue to manage trust assets, even though they are placed in a revocable living trust, or he may turn complete management over to the trustee. The creation of the trust during the grantor's lifetime allows the grantor to study the management of the assets by the trustee to be sure that the trustee will handle them in the proper manner after the grantor's death. The management of property placed in a revocable living trust is uninterrupted at death. Such continuity may be particularly important when the property managed is a closely held business needing constant attention. By placing property owned in other states in a revocable living trust, probate within those states may be avoided.

THE IRREVOCABLE TRUST

The irrevocable trust is one which the grantor cannot revoke or alter. The grantor of the trust has given up the right to change his mind, and has relinquished control over the trust property either permanently, or for some specific period of time. An irrevocable trust may be created during the lifetime of the grantor, or it may result from a revocable trust which, by its terms, becomes irrevocable upon the grantor's death. A testamentary trust (one created by a person's will) is obviously irrevocable since it cannot be changed after the testator's death.

Why Irrevocable Trusts?

Since the irrevocable trust, by definition, involves a more permanent form of arrangement than the revocable trust, it seems wise to again consider at least briefly some basic background information concerning trusts. A trust is simply a device in which the legal title to property and the right to control it, are separated from the right to receive the benefits from it.

Historically, the need for such a separation between benefits from property, and management of such property, arose from the plight of the man with property (in former times, unlike today, when men owned most of the wealth) who wanted to make provision for his family or friends, but feared giving property directly to them because of his distrust of their inexperience in financial management, or their irresponsibility. He solved this problem by placing the legal title and management of the property in the hands of a third party (the trustee) whom he considered responsible. He then stipulated the manner in which the benefits were to be paid to, or applied for the benefit of, family members (the beneficiaries).

The assurance of proper financial management and protection of beneficiaries is probably the most important reason for the existence of trusts. Who should be selected as trustee to exercise this management responsibility and care for the needs of the family? This decision is much more important in an irrevocable trust than in a revocable trust since the irrevocable trust cannot be changed. Imagine naming the smart and savvy brother-in-law, who later divorces your sister and is awarded the Big Bum award — and who now has control over the family estate. Sometimes a person wanting to create a trust has confidence in the judgment and managing abilities of a relative, a friend, or a business associate. But such a person is not always available. Even if such a person is available, that person may die, or become disabled, or be unwilling to serve due to other time commitments.

The unavailability of a reliable and experienced individual to serve as trustee may dictate the appointment of a bank or trust company. Almost every bank of substantial size now has a trust department. Although their skill in managing property and investments varies, the close governmental supervision of bank trust department activities assures certain capabilities and inspires confidence in the integrity of banks as trustees. Grantors often find the combination of a bank and an individual as co-trustees is desirable.

In addition to sound financial management, a trust offers its grantor an opportunity for great flexibility in carrying out objectives for the care of the beneficiaries. Many variations are available. A classic pattern is for one beneficiary to receive all of the income for life, with the remaining trust assets at death to be distributed to another beneficiary. The income, as well as the trust remainder, can be divided among several beneficiaries if that is desirable, and termination of the trust can be designated to occur at the time of a beneficiary's death, or upon the occurrence of a specified event other than death. For example, a father might create a trust providing for distribution of the income and principal among his children according to their respective needs from time to time, until the youngest child attains age 25. At that time, the trust could terminate, and the remaining trust assets could be divided equally among the children. The variations are limitless.

Even with all the possibilities open to the grantor of a trust, it must be recognized that the circumstances which inspire our decisions today may change during the term of the trust. The perfect plan of distribution which we create today may become the straightjacket of tomorrow when unexpected events occur. For example, a trust which irrevocably provides for the equal division of income between two children may seem unfortunate, in retrospect, if one child accumulates wealth and has great income, while the other child becomes incapacitated and incapable of supporting himself. The recognition of our inability to see into the future requires drafting the irrevocable trust in a manner which gives the trustee the ability to meet the unexpected.

One method of allowing for the unexpected is to give the trustee discretion in distributing income and principal from the trust. The trust agreement may provide that the trustee can either accumulate income in the trust or distribute it to a beneficiary, depending upon the circumstances at the time. The most obvious need for such a provision is in a trust for minors. The amount of money needed for the support of a minor varies greatly as the child develops through the years. Usually, the decision of how much income to distribute each year can be made best as events unfold. The grantor can specify in the instrument the criteria to be used by the trustee in making distributions (for example, a provision that the trust provide for the education, health, maintenance and support of the beneficiary, according to the same standard of living enjoyed by the beneficiary during the grantor's lifetime). Alternatively, there may be sufficient confidence in the trustee to follow the course of allowing the trustee complete discretion. If a beneficiary has developed a drug or alcohol addiction, the trustee may be authorized to require testing of the beneficiary before making distributions. If a child is lazy, the trustee might be authorized to match income earned by the child each year — the more the child earns, the more the child will receive from the trust.

The trustee can also be granted limited or broad power to decide who among a group of beneficiaries will receive distributions of income and principal, and how much each member of the group will receive. This permits making the decision at the time of the distribution, rather than trying to make it in advance.

Permanent or Long-Term Trusts

Usually, the only reason to make a trust irrevocable is to remove the asset transferred to the trust from the grantor's estate. Such trusts are an alternative to an outright gift. If the trust is properly drawn, the trust asset will be removed from the grantor's taxable estate, and thus effect the same tax savings as outright gifts do. However, the grantor may not reserve any right to modify the terms of the trust, and may not receive income or principal from the trust. Otherwise, the grantor will still be considered to be the owner of the trust property for tax purposes, in spite of the irrevocable nature of the trust gift. The safest course from a tax standpoint is for the grantor to rely entirely on an independent trustee, and retain no administrative power over the trust.

One type of tax savings gained from using trusts is the income tax savings afforded by sprinkling trusts and multiple trusts. The sprinkling trust is a trust under which an independent trustee, often a bank, is given broad discretion to either accumulate income in the trust, or distribute the income among a number of beneficiaries. A trust of this type is a taxpayer itself, paying tax on its accumulated income.

Because of the graduated income tax rates, a given amount of income will incur the least amount of tax if it is spread among a maximum number of taxpayers. Suppose, for example, a man with a wife and three children dies and leaves his property in three separate trusts — one for each child. The income and principal of each trust can be accumulated or distributed either to the child for whom the trust is held, or to the child's mother. If the mother's separate property proves inadequate for her support, the income from the trusts can be distributed to her. However, if she has adequate funds apart from the children's trusts in any given year, then the income can be retained in the trusts, where it may be taxed at a lower rate, or, some or all of the income can be distributed to the children, if they need it. The children may be in a lower tax bracket than the mother or the trusts. The important point is that the income can be divided among the mother, the three trusts, and the three children — seven taxpayers — to provide maximum tax advantages while taking care of their needs.

In creating long-term permanent trusts, the grantor should take care in selecting the trustee, and in providing for successor trustees. Care should also be taken to give the trustee or trustees broad enough management and investment powers to permit flexible administration of the trust in today's complex economic environment.

Section 2503(c) Trusts

The section 2503(c) trust is a form of a permanent trust designed specifically as an alternative to an outright gift to a minor beneficiary. Chapter 9 of this book discusses the rules relating to the tax consequences of lifetime gifts. The tax laws provide for an annual gift tax exclusion (this amount is indexed for inflation, but is $11,000 at the time this book is being written). Gifts of less than the annual exclusion amount are not taxable to the donor or the donee, and are not required to be reported to the Internal Revenue Service. However, the tax law allows the annual exclusion only for gifts "other than gifts of future interest in property." This means that it is possible to give the annual exclusion amount each year to any number of beneficiaries, so long as it is not a gift of a future interest. A transfer in trust, with the trustee having discretion with respect to the distribution of income and principal, is usually treated as a future interest (rather than a present interest) for purposes of the gift tax. The annual exclusion would not, therefore, be available for gifts to a trust.

Section 2503(c) of the Internal Revenue Code provides an exception to this rule if the property and the income from it may be used for the benefit of the trust beneficiary while under 21 years of age, and to the extent not so used, will pass outright to the beneficiary upon attaining age 21 (or be payable to the beneficiary's estate if death occurs before reaching age 21). For large gifts, a parent may not want a child to receive the trust upon reaching age 21. Section 2503(c) provides a solution to this problem by allowing the trust to continue beyond the beneficiary's twenty-first birthday, so long as the beneficiary is given the option of demanding that the trustee terminate the trust upon reaching age 21. If the transfer is to qualify for the annual exclusion under Section 2503(c), the trust instrument may not contain any substantial restrictions on the use of the trust property for the benefit of the minor beneficiary.

Demand (Crummey) Trusts

Another type of permanent trust frequently used to qualify a gift for the annual gift tax exclusion is the "demand" or Crummey trust. This type of trust can be an alternative to the Section 2503(c) trust for the benefit of minor children, but it can also be used for qualifying gifts in trust for adults. Its most common use is in connection with gifts of life insurance policies (see Chapter 19 for more on this subject). These trusts are named after a taxpayer who had the misfortune of having the last name of Crummey, and who won an important case against the Internal Revenue Service in 1968. That case established the general principles now relied upon and approved in many rulings by the Internal Revenue Service. Basically, that case provides that the gift tax annual exclusion is allowed for gifts to a trust in which the trust beneficiary has the unlimited right to demand that the trustee distribute the gift directly to the beneficiary (in the form of a withdrawal power), rather than holding the gift in the trust. In order for the withdrawal power to qualify for the annual exclusion, the beneficiary must be given notice of the existence of the right, and have a reasonable time within which to exercise the power. The demand power is limited to gifts made during each calendar year, and the right to make withdrawals expires, or lapses, at the end of the specified period given in the notice (often at the end of 30 days, or at the end of each calendar year). To the extent a withdrawal is not demanded during the specified period of time, it may not be accumulated and exercised in a later year.

Summary

Irrevocable trusts, created either while living or by will, are extremely useful estate planning tools, both for tax and non-tax reasons. Large savings of both estate taxes and income taxes can be realized; but even more important, proper management of property, and provisions for effective security for one's family often can be assured only through trusts.

LIFE INSURANCE

Ownership of life insurance is a popular method of transferring wealth to family and other heirs without the necessity of formal probate, or the use of a will. It is, no doubt, one of the most commonly held, and yet widely misunderstood assets.

The Concept of Life Insurance

By and large, the general concept of life insurance is easy to understand. An insurance company (insurer) agrees with an individual (insured) to pay a sum of money, in one lump sum or over time, at the insured's death, whenever it occurs. The proceeds of the policy will be distributed directly to the beneficiary by virtue of the contractual obligation of the insurer, rather than through any other dispositive instrument of the insured like a will.

In exchange for the insurer's obligation to pay cash, the insured agrees to pay a periodic payment (premium) to the insurer in an amount which is mathematically, and actuarially, calculated to be sufficient to cover the death benefit, administration and overhead costs, commissions, and profits. The insurance company attempts to predict when its insureds are likely to die, how much profit they can make with each insured's premium payments over the years before death, and the costs associated with administering the policy. This, coupled with favorable tax laws on insurance company reserves, enables the insurer to provide substantial proceeds to the insured's beneficiaries, even if the individual dies shortly after taking out the policy.

The owner of the policy (policyholder) is often, but not necessarily, the insured. Sometimes the policyholder is also the beneficiary, or the beneficiary is a trust established for the benefit of the insured's family or heirs. The policyholder has the obligation to make the premium payments, as well as the power to decide, among other things, who the beneficiary will be, how the proceeds will be paid, and whether to borrow any cash value in the policy during the insured's life.

Types of Life Insurance Policies

Describing the types of insurance policies available today would require a full-length book. Even then, the description is apt to be incomplete, since new policies are continually being developed.

There are two primary categories of insurance contracts, with numerous variations available. They are ordinary life and term life insurance. An ordinary life insurance policy is a permanent contract with a level (non-increasing) cost to the purchaser, based upon the age and health of the insured at the time the policy is first issued. The insurer establishes a fixed price which contains a cost for the increasing risk of mortality, and a cost for the savings portion of the policy, known as cash surrender value. The cash surrender value portion is the excess charge which affords the insured the ability to maintain a level premium payment. Some ordinary life products require premium payments continually until death. Others are designed to be fully paid up at a specific age, or after a certain number of years. In recent years, the cash value of some policies has been capable of growing so rapidly through interest allocated, or dividends paid, by the insurer that the incremental value is sufficient to actually pay the next year's policy premium.

A term life insurance policy is a limited duration contract, which lasts only as long as the term prescribed in the policy, plus any permitted extensions or renewals. The term can vary, and the cost each year may increase, or may be set to remain level for the term of the policy. The contract can provide for automatic renewal, discretionary renewal, or non-renewal. Typically, the cost of these policies increases with each renewal as the risk of the insured's mortality increases. Since there is usually no cash value associated with these policies, the initial cost is substantially reduced. The temptation is to purchase term insurance since it is cheaper. However, a little know fact is that only about 2% of term policies ever end up paying a death benefit — and that is why they are so cheap — because the insurance company has developed techniques to determine about how long the insured will live, and assures that most insureds will die after the policy expires. Therefore, except where the insured is only needing to have a death benefit for a known period of time — until children finish college, or until other assets are expected to have grown to a sufficient amount to provide for family needs — permanent insurance may ultimately be a better product.

There are many variations of permanent and term insurance. Term insurance may be an annual renewable policy, which means that it expires each year and can be renewed only with the consent of the insurance company, or it may be a level term policy, which will remain in effect for the specified number of years at a set premium, which will not increase during the term.

When purchasing a term policy, it is important to make certain it has a clause which permits the insured to convert to a permanent policy at any time prior to the expiration of the term. In this way, if the insured later decides that a permanent policy would better serve the family or business needs, the policy can be changed, with the premium being increased to reflect the permanent cost for insurance at the then attained age of the insured. Policies with these provisions generally allow conversions to be made regardless of the health and insurability of the insured at that time.

Many variations of permanent life insurance also exist. Whole life is the oldest variation of permanent life, and offers the predictability of guaranteed premiums and insurability, but is also the most costly of all insurance. Guarantees come at a price. Universal life is similar to whole life, but has greater flexibility because the premiums cost is more closely tied to the investment performance of the insurance company. There is a minimum guaranteed interest rate in the policy, but this rate is typically lower than with whole life policies. The insured can often skip premiums from time to time, but this may eventually result in the policy becoming under funded, and placing the coverage in some jeopardy. Universal life policies, therefore, require more frequent attention. There are also many variations of universal life.

A more recent innovation by life insurance companies is the introduction of "survivorship life" or "second-to-die life insurance" policies. These policies have been designed primarily to fund federal estate tax obligations upon the death of the last of the spouses to die. As we have seen, most estate tax planning emphasizes the deferral of the tax until the death of the last spouse to die. Since it is impossible to determine in advance who the surviving spouse will be, the survivorship policy insures the lives of both the husband and wife, and pays the death benefit at the death of the last to die — the moment when the tax ultimately becomes due. In addition, since the insurance company is only paying the death benefit after the death of two insureds instead of one, the premium cost is usually much lower than insuring a single life.

The important thing to remember in purchasing life insurance is the need to consult an experienced life insurance agent who understands the various policy variations and can match the correct policy with your cash need objectives. Purchasing the wrong type of policy can be a terrible mistake.

Tax Treatment of Life Insurance

There are a variety of income, gift, and estate tax consequences that affect the purchase, ownership, and transfer of insurance policies, and the receipt of policy proceeds upon the death of the insured.

How Is the Beneficiary Taxed upon Receipt of Life Insurance Proceeds?

Generally, the proceeds payable by reason of an insured's death are not subject to income tax, regardless of whether the proceeds are paid to individual beneficiaries, or to the insured's estate. The main exception to this result arises from the "transfer for value" rule, which may apply when the insurance proceeds are received by a person who has purchased the policy from the original owner of the policy. This is a complicated rule which will most often be triggered in business arrangements.

What If the Insurance Proceeds are Paid over a Fixed Period of Time or in a Fixed Number of Installments?

The proceeds are still exempt from income tax, but any interest paid on the installments is taxable as ordinary income.

Are Premium Payments Deductible by the Policyholder or Taxable to Him?

A policy owned by an individual is considered a personal asset, and premium payments are deemed nondeductible personal expenses. Premiums paid by someone other than a policyholder, such as a parent, child, or friend, are considered a gift to the owner rather than income.

Premiums paid by an employer on a policy owned by an employee are considered taxable compensation to the employee, unless it is part of a qualified plan of group term insurance and the death benefit does not exceed $50,000.

Will the Proceeds of Life Insurance Be Subject to Federal Estate Tax?

If insurance proceeds are paid to or for the benefit of the insured's estate, the proceeds will be included in the insured's gross estate, and subject to death taxes. Where the insured retained any "incidents of ownership" over the policy, the proceeds will also be included in the insured's gross estate. The phrase "incidents of ownership" has specific meaning in the tax law. It refers to such powers as the right to designate the beneficiary of the death benefit, the right to determine the time and manner of payment of proceeds, the right to borrow on the cash surrender value, and the right to transfer the ownership of the policy to someone else.

Ownership of an insurance policy which is transferred by the insured to someone else within three years of the insured's death is automatically brought back into the insured's estate for death tax purposes. The reason for the transfer is irrelevant; the only issue is whether the transfer took place within three years of death. If so, the entire policy proceeds are included in the gross estate for estate tax purposes. However, if an insured transfers all incidents of ownership to a trust, or another person, more than three years prior to death, the death proceeds will not be taxable for income or estate tax purposes. Even more importantly, if a policy is initially applied for and owned by someone other than the insured, so that the insured never acquired any of the incidents of ownership, the death benefit will be excluded from the insured's estate for tax purposes, and the three year rule does not apply.

Are There Any Gift Taxes Required upon the Transfer of a Life Insurance Policy or Gratuitous Payment of Premiums?

A gift of an insurance policy occurs when the policyholder irrevocably transfers all incidents of ownership to another person for less than full and adequate consideration. If the transfer is revocable, or the donor retains incidents of ownership, then the gift is incomplete for gift tax purposes. It does not mean that the donee has no power over the policy transferred, only that a taxable gift has not occurred.

An insurance policy is valued at its fair market value as of the time of the gift. Such value will vary depending on the type of policy involved. An ordinary life policy is measured by its "interpolated terminal reserve value," roughly equivalent to its cash surrender value, plus any unearned premiums. A term life policy is usually worth only the amount of any unearned premiums. Payment of the premium by someone other than the owner of the policy results in a gift being made by the premium payer.

A very important tax trap to avoid is the situation where the non-insured owner of the policy causes the beneficiary to be someone else. For example, mother owns a policy on father's life and makes the children the beneficiaries. Upon father's death, mother will be treated as having gifted to the children the amount of the insurance death benefit.

Irrevocable Life Insurance Trusts

Since life insurance is frequently as asset of little lifetime benefit to the insured, it makes an ideal asset to gift in order to remove the death benefit from the estate for tax purposes. This is especially true where the addition of the death benefit to the value of other assets would cause an estate tax to become due, or would significantly increase the amount of such taxes.

A very important estate planning tool is the irrevocable life insurance trust. The person to be insured creates an irrevocable trust. The insured cannot be the trustee, or a beneficiary of the trust, nor may the insured reserve any right to direct the investment of trust assets, or dictate the use of the trust assets for the use of the family members named as beneficiaries. The trust is typically funded only with the insurance policy (or policies), and enough cash to pay the initial premium. Each year, additional cash gifts are made to pay the current year's premium obligation.

The trust provides that, at the death of the insured, the policy proceeds will be held by the trustee for the benefit of the surviving spouse and children. Income is paid periodically to the spouse, and principal is available for the spouse's health, support, and maintenance. The trust can provide for loans to be made to the deceased insured's estate to facilitate payment of federal estate taxes, and avoid the need to liquidate assets.

When the surviving spouse dies, the remaining proceeds can be distributed outright to the children, or held in trust until the children reach sufficient age and maturity to responsibly handle their portion of the funds. Again, the trust can loan money to the surviving spouse's estate, so that the estate has sufficient cash to pay death taxes, and other expenses, without having to sell assets.

The unique tax advantages of this device include avoiding death taxes when the insured dies (since the policy was either initially acquired by the trust, or was gifted to the irrevocable trust more than three years before death). In addition, a properly drafted trust will eliminate taxation of the remaining trust assets in the estate of the surviving spouse, since that spouse will have been provided the right to use the trust assets without being treated as the owner of such assets. Finally, the trust may even provide that the assets remain in the trust for the benefit of the children for their lives, and ultimately be distributed to grandchildren, without being taxed in the children's estates. This is called a generation-skipping trust.

Summary
The absence of any death taxes, income taxes, or significant gift taxes on the insurance policy proceeds makes the irrevocable life insurance trust an attractive planning tool. But such advantages are available only to a carefully designed, and artfully drafted, instrument. Community property rules do not prevent, but may certainly complicate, an effective plan. The advice of knowledgeable tax advisors is a necessity.

THE DURABLE POWER OF ATTORNEY

*My interest is in the future because I am going to spend
the rest of my life there.*
— Charles F. Kettering

Most of this book is concerned with the subjects of death and taxes. Although these are the inevitable circumstances with which most estate planning deals, there is also the troubling possibility of a lifetime disability, making it impossible for the disabled person to effectively manage his assets and affairs. For some, this is where they may spend their future. There are procedures established under the Colorado Probate Code for the appointment of a guardian or conservator to step in and take over these responsibilities.

Under Colorado law, a "guardian" is a person appointed by the court to be responsible for the personal affairs of a minor or disabled adult individual. A "conservator" is a person designated by the court to have responsibility for the financial affairs of a minor or disabled adult individual. It is possible that the same person might be designated to serve as both the guardian and the conservator, but these functions can be put in the hands of different individuals, or even in the hands of professional fiduciaries. A guardianship or conservatorship requires a court proceeding, and results in avoidable cost and inflexibility.

One way to avoid the problems resulting from lifetime disability is the creation of a revocable living trust, into which all of an individual's assets are transferred. (See Chapter 17 for further discussion). Such a trust is not subject to court supervision, and can provide for continued management of the assets by the named trustee during any period of disability or incompetency. Provisions can also be made for the continued care of the disabled person's family by using the trust property. However, there may be many situations where the use of a revocable living trust is not desirable, or efficient, because the size of the estate is not large enough to justify the cost and complications of a trust. The use of a power of attorney may be the best way to protect against disability in these cases.

What Is a Power of Attorney?

The use of powers of attorney is not limited to estate planning. For hundreds of years, people have been using powers of attorney to authorize relatives, or business associates, to transact business. The person granting the power (usually called a "principal") signs a written instrument giving another individual (usually called the "agent" or the "attorney-in-fact") the authority to transact certain matters.

A general power of attorney gives the agent the ability to do anything and everything the principal could do. It is a complete and unlimited grant of authority. On the other hand, a special, or limited, power of attorney is designed to give the agent the authority to transact only certain specified acts, and there is no authority to do anything which is not necessary to accomplish the specific activity listed in the power of attorney.

A power of attorney may be of unlimited time duration, and could continue to be valid until the death of the principal, or until revoked in writing. On the other hand, the power may specifically be exercisable only until a stated date, or for a certain period of time. All powers of attorney terminate upon the death of the principal.

Although the power of attorney can be very helpful in a large number of circumstances, it is also a powerful and destructive weapon in the wrong hands. Therefore, it is essential to get good legal advice about the need for a power of attorney, and how it should be structured. There is always a real problem in attempting to revoke a power of attorney which has no time limits. Even though such a power can be terminated in writing by the principal, such a termination is ineffective with regard to transactions between the attorney-in-fact and third persons, if the third person has no actual knowledge of the revocation. As a result, a person holding an apparently valid power of attorney can create many financial and legal obligations which are fully binding upon the principal, even though the principal has made every effort to terminate the power. The only certain way to terminate a power of attorney is to physically retrieve it and destroy it.

What Is a Durable Power of Attorney?

The problem with the ordinary power of attorney has historically been that it does not protect the principal against the lifetime disability problem. In many states, and in Colorado prior to 1974, a power of attorney was, by law, automatically revoked upon the disability of the principal. The purpose of this rule was to protect a disabled principal from abuse at the hands of the attorney-in-fact, resulting from the disabled principal's inability to effectively revoke the power. Most laypersons were unaware of this rule.

The Colorado Probate Code specifically permits a power of attorney to be made "durable," so that it survives the disability or incapacity of the principal. To be durable, the power of attorney must only contain the words, "This power of attorney shall not be affected by the disability of the principal."

It is also possible to have a power of attorney become effective only in the event the principal becomes disabled at some future time, by having the power of attorney contain the words, "This power of attorney shall become effective upon the disability of the principal." The problem with this approach is that the agent, before using the power of attorney, would need satisfactory evidence that the principal was disabled or incompetent. Otherwise, third parties would be reluctant or unwilling to accept the agent's authority. This might result in the necessity of having a court determination of the incapacity of the principal, so that an appropriate court order could be obtained as evidence of the effectiveness of the power.

What Powers Should be Granted?

The contents of the power of attorney will depend upon the expected needs of the principal. Business and financial management are the most common powers to be included. These would include the power to buy and sell assets, to manage a business interest, to borrow money and otherwise deal with banks, to handle life insurance matters, and gain access to a safe deposit box. Colorado has a statutory power of attorney, which is a form available from Bradford Publishing Company, or an attorney. The statutory form enumerates a checklist of powers, and the person making the power can initial those powers to be granted.

Health Care Powers of Attorney

The typical durable power of attorney is designed to provide for the management of financial and legal matters. Equally important is the need to provide for medical emergencies. The health care power of attorney names a trusted family member to sign hospital consents, employ physicians, and otherwise take care of the health needs of the principal during any time the principal is unable to do so. This form is so important that federal law now requires all hospitals to inquire of patients, prior to admission, if they have prepared such a power. A suitable form is available at all Colorado hospitals, Bradford Publishing Company, or may be prepared by an attorney.

Delegation of Parental Powers

There is a particularly useful provision in the Colorado Probate Code allowing a parent to delegate his parental responsibilities to another person on a temporary basis. A parent may be going on an extended vacation and may desire to leave a minor child in the temporary custody of friends or other family members. In the absence of the parent, it might be necessary to make decisions with regard to school activities of the child, or medical care and treatment in the event of an emergency. Another common situation is where a minor child goes to visit a grandparent, or other relative, during summer vacation, and the grandparent might have a need to make emergency medical decisions in the event of an accident or illness.

The parent of a minor child can execute a power of attorney, and delegate to another person any of his powers regarding the care, custody, or property of the minor child. The only exception is that a power may not be given to consent to the marriage, or adoption, of the minor child. This parental power of attorney may not be given for a period exceeding 12 months. This statute can be very helpful in a wide variety of circumstances.

Summary

As we live longer, it becomes increasingly likely that there will be some sort of emergency affecting our ability to manage financial matters for ourselves or to make medical decisions. In the absence of a power of attorney which has been given to a trusted friend or family member, it may be necessary to have a court determination of incompetency resulting in a protracted and costly guardianship and conservatorship. Preserving your wealth requires that such concerns be anticipated. When considering the person to be given a power of attorney, use care that they are completely trustworthy since the power of attorney is the equivalent of a blank check. It is a valuable tool in the right hands. It is an invitation to disaster in the wrong hands.

MY FARM OR BUSINESS

Many have devoted their lives and energies to developing a successful business enterprise. This business operation may be a sole proprietorship, a partnership, or a closely held corporation. The business involved may include everything from farming to manufacturing. It may employ two persons or 2000. Whether the business can survive the death of the individual who was the original spark behind the company will depend largely on the amount of planning that has been done for the protection of the business.

Most businessmen are so preoccupied with daily business problems that they fail to realize that all the benefits of their lifetime of effort may be lost after death, unless proper preparations have been made for the orderly continuation, or disposition, of these business interests. It is an unfortunate statistic that most family businesses do not survive beyond two generations.

What are some of the basic problems which should be considered in planning for the protection of a family business at the time of the business owner's death?

Sale or Continued Operation

The first consideration that must be made after the business owner's death is whether to sell the business or continue its operations. This important decision will provide the framework in planning for the protection of the family. If there are no family members who are interested in continuing the business, the planning considerations are very different than in cases where children have become an important part of business operations and intend to make the business their life effort.

Any business, regardless of its legal form, can become paralyzed following the death of an owner. Uninterrupted production during this period is usually difficult because the individual who has been responsible for the daily operations and decisions is gone. Banking relationships may come to a halt, and borrowing for business needs suspended, because the bank relied on the business skill of the deceased owner and is unwilling to trust the relatively inexperienced children. An orderly plan for the transfer of operational and managerial control, or immediate sale, is essential to insure the realization of maximum values for the owner's family.

A sole proprietorship is a business in which a single individual owns all of the assets. If the owner dies, the personal representative of the estate will usually be under a duty to liquidate the business, without delay, to preserve the present value of the assets, unless provisions have been made in the will for the continuation of the business.

If the business is one in which the owner's personal services were the primary income-producing factor (such as a physician, accountant, or lawyer), it is probably advisable to arrange for a sale of the business assets at death. Unless there is a prospective purchaser for the business, there will usually be little value at death. Care should be exercised in specifying which assets used in the business are to be sold, and some specific provisions should be made for payment of the business liabilities.

However, if the business is one in which the owner's capital investment was the primary income-producing factor, it is generally in the best interests of the family to arrange for a continuation of the business. This may be done by directing the personal representative of the will to continue the business, and by providing broad powers to permit prompt action in exercising sound business judgment. Alternatively, the will may direct that the business be operated in trust. The will should provide for an immediate transfer and delivery of the business assets to insure continuity of operations.

Unless the partnership agreement provides otherwise, a partnership is usually terminated on the death of a partner, and the surviving partners are required by law to liquidate the business, and make an accounting to the deceased partner's estate. It is possible, by making appropriate provisions in the will, to continue the partnership operations with the decedent's estate or beneficiaries. The deceased partner's will should include specific directions with respect to the continuance or liquidation of the partnership.

Partnership agreements can be drawn to protect the deceased partner's interest from forced sale, or involuntary liquidation. The partners should decide during their lifetimes whether to sell their interests at death, or provide for the continued participation by their families. The decision to sell or continue the business operations upon the death of a partner should be incorporated into the partnership agreement and each partner's will, in order to protect both the surviving partners and the decedent's family.

The ownership of a corporate business enterprise by an individual is evidenced by stock ownership. The decision of sale or continued operation of a decedent's corporation is complex. The general considerations in selling a sole proprietorship are equally applicable here. If personal services are a major factor, a sale at death is desirable, while the business should be continued if a capital investment is a major factor. In addition it is necessary to consider other factors.

Liquidity

Death creates a need for cash. Many businessmen operate on credit for extensive periods of time, and are constantly rearranging their business financing to provide working capital for personal needs. This source of cash usually ends upon death. Yet funds must be provided for the family's living expenses, as well as for debts and various taxes.

If the business, or its assets, are to be sold, the terms of the sale should be structured to insure the availability of necessary funds for debts and taxes. If the business is to be continued at death, a plan must exist to provide for the availability of sufficient funds for payment of debts and taxes, to make sure the business can continue and does not have to be sold.

With a sole proprietorship, cash may be generated from the sale of specific assets, the maintenance of life insurance, or the borrowing of necessary funds by the personal representative with appropriate directions and powers in the will.

In a partnership, when the partners have so agreed, taxes may be paid with withdrawals from the deceased partner's capital account. Current partnership earnings may also be available for a period of time after death for this purpose. It is important to designate these payments as a continuation of income participation by the deceased partner's estate, so that such payments are not mistaken for payments in purchase of the decedent's interest. The partners should plan in advance to finance the purchase of a decedent's interest, as well as the continued operation of the business during this difficult transition period.

Corporate Redemption Under Section 303

Naturally, the owners of a closely held corporation may experience great difficulty in raising the cash needed at death because of the absence of a market for their securities. Distributions from the corporation to the deceased shareholder's estate may result in taxable dividends. However, under certain conditions, Section 303 of the Internal Revenue Code permits a corporation to redeem a decedent's stock to fund funeral expenses, death taxes, and other costs of administering the decedent's estate, without dividend tax consequences. The corporation may thereby provide the needed cash from accumulated earnings without adverse income tax consequences to the decedent's estate, so long as the redemption price of the stock is equal to its estate tax value. Purchase of the shares by the corporation will not result in capital gains tax to the estate, since the estate receives a stepped-basis equal to the fair market value of the stock on the date of death.

To qualify for this income tax benefit, the value of the decedent's stock in the closely held corporation must exceed 35% of the decedent's adjusted gross estate. The adjusted gross estate is generally the gross value of the estate minus the debts, losses, and funeral and administrative expenses. Stock in two or more businesses may be aggregated together to meet this 35% requirement, if a decedent owned 20% or more of the value in each business.

The redemption of shares by the corporation may be made for cash, a promissory note, or other corporate property. Moreover, the funds or property withdrawn need not be actually used to pay the death tax, funeral, and administrative expenses, but can be used for other cash needs of the estate.

Deferral and Installment Payment of Estate Tax

The estate may also qualify for an installment payment of that portion of the federal estate tax attributable to the value of a closely held business. If the value of the decedent's interest in a closely held business exceeds 35% of the adjusted gross estate, Section 6166 of the Internal Revenue Code allows the personal representative to elect to pay the portion of the estate tax attributable to the business in up to ten equal installments. Two or more business interests can be combined to qualify for the 35% requirement, if the decedent owned 20% or more of the total value of each such business.

The first installment of tax is not due until on or before five years and nine months after the date of death, and successive installments are due annually thereafter. The estate may pay interest only for the first five years, followed by ten annual installments of principal and interest. One of the really tremendous advantages of this provision of the Code is that interest on the deferred estate tax on the first $1 million dollars of estate tax liability attributable to the qualifying closely held business interest is at only a 2% rate. Interest on the balance of the deferred tax not qualifying for the 2% rate is also at a preferential rate.

Generally, most businesses will qualify; however, certain kinds of activities, such as management of passive investments will not. The requirements for qualification should be carefully reviewed with counsel.

After a family begins the installment payments, there are still some concerns. Acceleration of the unpaid federal estate tax can occur if more than 50% of the business is sold or disposed of during the installment period. Failure to pay either the interest, or principal, on any installment will also trigger acceleration of the remaining tax. The IRS may also impose a tax lien on the business assets, making it difficult to borrow working capital.

Special Use Valuation for Farms and Business Real Property

Property is valued at its "highest and best use" for purposes of assessing the federal estate tax. (See Chapter 3 for additional information on valuation.) A problem encountered in recent times exists when a family farming operation is surrounded by commercial or residential development, resulting in an inflated value for the farm real estate far beyond its economic value as a farming operation. This can have devastating results upon the death of a farm owner, whose estate is now confronted with the need to pay estate taxes based on these inflated real estate values. The requirement to pay estate taxes within nine months of the date of death, coupled with the lack of earning capacity and liquidity existing in many farming operations, can force the sale of the family business and the destruction of a desirable life style by the surviving family members.

Section 2032A of the Internal Revenue Code was enacted in recognition of this problem, and allows an optional method of valuing qualified real property which is a farm, or is used in a closely-held business, if such property forms a substantial part of the decedent's estate. This optional method of valuation is designed to approximate the actual use value, rather than the inflated use which might otherwise be dictated in a highest and best use environment.

This real property must be included in the decedent's gross estate, and must be "qualified real property" applied to a "qualified use" that passes to a "qualified heir." Proper planning is critical to enjoy this valuable relief provision. The property must represent at least 50% of the value of the decedent's adjusted gross estate. The estate is only allowed a maximum reduction in valuation of $750,000 (indexed for inflation), from the "highest and best use" value. In 2003 the maximum reduction in value available is $820,000.

Qualified Family-Owned Business Interest Deduction

Similar to the special use valuation rules for real estate under Section 2032A, there is a special deduction for the value of a qualified family-owned business interest (QFOBI) under Section 2057 of the Code. In very general terms, if the value of a QFOBI owned by a decedent exceeds 50% of the value of the estate a deduction can be applied to offset the value of the QFOBI, reducing the tax attributable to the QFOBI. The combination of the QFOBI deduction and the exempt amount may not exceed $1.3 million. Although when originally enacted in 1997 the maximum available QFOBI deduction was $675,000, because of the increase in the exempt amount, the maximum QFOBI credit available in 2003 is $300,000. Additionally, because of the increase in the exempt amount in 2004 to $1.5 million, the QFOBI deduction will not be available to estates of decedents who die after December 31, 2003. However, under current law, the QFOBI deduction may become available again in 2011, when the current estate tax law is scheduled to sunset, and the exempt amount is scheduled to revert to $1,000,000. The amount of the deduction and the rules for qualification are complicated, and the advice of qualified tax counsel should be obtained.

Buy-Sell Agreements

This type of business agreement is a contract which provides for the purchase and sale of a deceased business owner's interest, whether a sole proprietorship, partnership, or corporation. The contract is used to protect the surviving family from forced sales, and depressed prices, while protecting the continuing owners or operators of the business from the interference of those in the decedent's family who are not active in the business.

Buy-sell agreements may include provisions for funding the purchase price with life insurance, and thereby assure that the cash will be available to quickly liquidate the decedent's interest in the business enterprise. These buy-sell provisions may be as broad, and varied, as the imagination of the business planner.

Parties to a buy-sell agreement may include present owners of the business, or may include employees, or other persons not currently a part of the business operations, who have an interest in acquiring the business at some future time. A sole proprietor may look to certain key employees who may be interested in taking over the farm or business. The same considerations would apply to one who is the only shareholder of a closely held corporation. Where there is more than one owner, the other owners may agree to purchase the decedent's interest. A competitor may also be interested in participating in a buy-sell agreement. There are several varieties of buy-sell agreements. Depending on the type of buy-sell utilized, there are different income tax consequences to the surviving business owners which must be considered in structuring the transaction. Without getting into the details, a cross-purchase agreement is often a better tax choice for the surviving business owner.

The Cross-Purchase Agreement

A cross-purchase agreement is between the owners of the business, and obligates the estate of a deceased owner to sell the decedent's interest to the remaining owners, who in turn are obligated to purchase the decedent's interest from the estate. The parties to this agreement are the individual owners, and not the partnership or corporation itself.

The cross-purchase agreement presents some potential problems. First, the surviving owners may find it very difficult to personally raise the funds necessary to purchase the decedent's interest. An installment sale can alleviate this problem to some extent. Life insurance policies that pay proceeds to the surviving owners on the decedent's death are also an alternative, but each business owner must maintain a life insurance policy on the life of each other owner. Where there are many owners, this creates the need for many insurance policies, and this can be both costly and confusing.

The Corporate Redemption Agreement

Many businesses select the "entity purchase" or "redemption" agreement, in which the business entity (partnership or closely-held corporation) agrees to purchase the interest of a retiring, or deceased owner. Corporate funds can then be used to purchase the interest of the decedent. A corporate redemption can be funded through life insurance, with only one policy needed on the life of each owner, in contrast to the multiplicity of policies required in the cross-purchase agreement.

Setting Estate Tax Values

One of the big problems of the closely, or privately held, business is the determination of the appropriate value to be included in the decedent's estate for federal estate tax purposes. Understandably, the personal representative of the estate of the deceased owner tends to want to appraise the value of assets at the lower end of their range of values, in order to minimize the estate tax consequences. On the other hand, the Internal Revenue Service, being suspicious of this tendency on the part of the estate and surviving family members, will tend to select the higher end of the range of values. Many costly tax disputes center around this question of valuation.

A properly drafted buy-sell agreement will often establish the value of the business for federal estate tax purposes, and eliminate costly tax litigation. The principal requirements for a valid agreement acceptable to the Internal Revenue Service are different for related business owners, than for unrelated business owners. This is due to the, perhaps justifiable, concern by the IRS, that such agreements will be used by family members merely to reduce tax liability, and will be without any real economic justification.

With respect to buy-sell agreements between unrelated persons, the principal requirements are: (1) lifetime restrictions upon sale or transfer of the business interest without the prior consent of the other business owners, (2) a mandatory obligation on the part of the estate to sell the business interest at death, and (3) a determinable purchase price contained in the agreement. It is immaterial whether the price determined under the agreement is payable in a lump sum or by installments.

To be effective in setting the estate tax value of a business owned by family members, the buy-sell agreement must satisfy six requirements: (1) the agreement must be a bona fide business arrangement, (2) the agreement must not be a device to transfer property to members of the decedent's family for less than full and adequate consideration in money or money's worth, (3) the agreement must have terms that are comparable to similar agreements entered into by person's in arms-length transactions, (4) the agreement must restrict transfer of the business interest, both during the decedent's life, and on the decedent's death, (5) the decedent's estate must be bound by the agreement to sell the business interest at the price fixed in the agreement, and (6) the selling price must be fixed, or calculable, according to a formula or another reasonable method.

The Family Limited Partnership

The family limited partnership has become a popular estate planning tool. The main advantages of this entity are: (1) the protection of property in the partnership from the claims of judgment creditors or bankruptcy claims, (2) the ability to gift partnership units to children at a reduced or discounted value, (3) the shifting of future appreciation on partnership assets to children, and thereby reducing the future value of the parent's estate, and (4) the ability of parents to transfer most of a family business, or investment asset, to children while still maintaining control of the asset.

Let's assume a person decides to form a family limited partnership for estate planning purposes. That person would typically begin by transferring the selected property to a partnership consisting of that person and his children. In a limited partnership, there are two classes of partners. The general partner (which would usually be the person who forms the partnership) retains complete control over all partnership matters, regardless of the size of the general partnership interest. Although the general partner in a traditional limited partnership has unlimited liability for actions taken on behalf of the partnership, Colorado has adopted a variation called a limited liability limited partnership, in which the general partner has no personal liability. To be recognized as a limited liability limited partnership, the partnership must be registered as such with the Colorado Secretary of State.

The limited partners of a limited partnership are treated merely as investors and have no voice whatsoever in the management or investment decisions of the partnership. Since the limited partners have no management rights, they have no liability for partnership matters, except to the extent of their actual investment in the partnership. In other words, their personal non-partnership assets are not subject to liabilities incurred by the partnership. Any income of the partnership would be distributed, and taxed, to the general and limited partners in proportion to their relative partnership interests. The decision to make or withhold distributions of income is in the sole discretion of the general partner.

The actual steps in implementing the partnership are important, and must be carefully followed. The person initiating formation of the partnership, typically a parent, and his children first sign the partnership agreement. The parent would initially be both a general partner and a limited partner. The children would only be limited partners. The parent and the children would each initially contribute a nominal amount of cash (e.g. $1,000 each). The parent would then transfer assets to the partnership, directing that a small percentage of those assets (e.g. 10%) would be allocated to the parent's general partnership interest, and the balance (90%) would be allocated to the parent's limited partnership interest. The parent would then gift all or a portion of the parent's limited partnership interest to the children.

Ordinarily, when a person transfers appreciated assets to a partnership in exchange for a partnership interest, there is no income tax consequence for that transfer. However, if the partnership is deemed to be an "investment company," then the transfer of assets to the partnership would be treated as a sale, with resulting capital gains taxed to the transferor. An "investment company" may exist where more than 80% of the value of the assets is readily marketable securities. However, it is usually possible to avoid this problem with careful planning.

There are several estate planning advantages to forming a family limited partnership. First, although a person may gift all or most of the value of the partnership to the children, that person still retains control because of his rights as the general partner. Second, the person is able to discount the value of the gifts because of the lack of control, and the lack of marketability, of the children's limited partnership interests. The discount could range from 15% to 50% or more, depending upon the structuring of the partnership agreement. In order to justify the higher discounts, it is advisable to employ a firm which specializes in valuing these partnership rights. In addition, their input would be valuable in structuring the restrictions and other conditions in the partnership agreement which would enhance the discount. Illustration 21-1 demonstrates the formation and gifting strategy of a typical family limited partnership.

Illustration 21-1

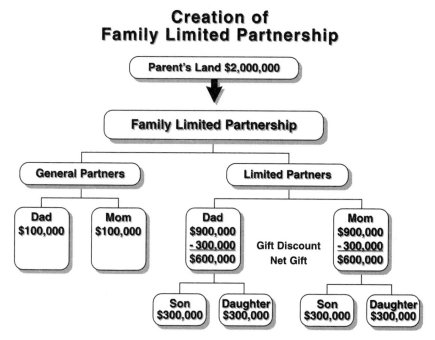

Creation of Family Limited Partnership

The disadvantages of the family limited partnership are primarily the costs of forming the partnership, appraising the value of and transferring the assets, and obtaining the valuation of the appropriate gifting discount. The additional record keeping and tax returns to be filed, and the loss of some of the income on the assets contributed to the partnership should also be considered. Since the partnership is a new tax entity, it must file income tax returns each year. As indicated, each partner is taxed on, and is ordinarily entitled to, distribution of their proportionate share of the net partnership income. The general partner could, and probably should, receive some compensation for acting as the general partner, and this amount would be deducted before determining the distributable net income of the partners. Assets contributed to the partnership retain the donor part-ner's income tax basis for computing capital gains upon a sale by the partnership.

Summary

There are no cure-all substitutes for thorough business planning to preserve the value of a farm or business at the owner's death. Nor is there a single device by which all problems created at death can be easily resolved. A well considered plan, which studies each of the problems peculiar to the business operation of the individual, is essential to preserve and protect the value of the business at death.

THE "LIVING WILL" AND OTHER
HEALTH CARE DIRECTIVES

The greatest tragedy is indifference.
— Red Cross slogan

Background of the "Living Will"

With the advances in medical treatment over the last several years, there has been an increasing controversy over the right to die when a patient has reached the point where death is imminent and inevitable. Although medical science can keep an individual in a state of almost perpetual vegetation, many individuals do not wish to have life sustained through the use of extraordinary techniques. Unfortunately, at the time when a patient is undergoing life-sustaining treatment, the patient is unable to express the patient's desires, because a coma usually accompanies these conditions.

Various organizations, such as the Society for the Right To Die, have lobbied vigorously for many years to persuade states to legislate the ability of patients to make a decision regarding this issue while they are still healthy and competent. This has been an emotional issue which involves religious, social, legal, and medical issues.

Most states have enacted statutes which recognize a person's ability to express their desires in regard to extraordinary medical care in the event of a terminal illness or injury. Colorado has enacted a statute called the Colorado Medical Treatment Act, which was signed into law on May 9, 1985. This law is patterned on similar statutes in other states, with various provisions peculiar to Colorado.

Since the acceptable provisions of a living will vary somewhat from state, it is important to have a living will which is clearly valid in the state where you reside. Living wills do not apply to emergency medical care, or to any form or treatment except artificial life support.

Colorado Law Regarding "Living Wills"

Under the Colorado statute, any competent adult may execute a written declaration (also referred to as a living will) directing that life-sustaining procedures be withheld or withdrawn in the event of a terminal condition, and if the person is either unconscious or otherwise incapable, of deciding whether medical treatment should be accepted or rejected. In the case of a declaration signed by a pregnant patient, if a medical evaluation determines that the fetus could probably be delivered alive, then any such written declaration is invalid. The declaration must be executed before two witnesses. However, the declaration need not necessarily be in the precise form described in the statute.

If the patient is physically unable to sign a declaration, the statute permits it to be signed by some other person in the patient's presence, and at the patient's direction. Neither the witnesses, nor a person signing a declaration on behalf of a physically disabled patient can be the attending physician, an employee of the attending physician, an employee of the institution in which the patient is hospitalized, or a person who could benefit from the estate of the patient at death.

There is a rather complicated procedure to be followed by the attending physician when presented with such a declaration. The attending physician, and at least one other physician, must both determine that the patient's medical condition is terminal. The attending physician then has certain requirements about notifying the patient's family members. If those family members do not challenge the declaration within forty-eight hours after the physician has signed a certificate of terminal condition, then all life-sustaining procedures are to be withdrawn or withheld, pursuant to the terms of the declaration. Any physician who acts in accordance with the declaration is exempted from any civil or criminal liability as a result of the decision to suspend medical procedures.

In order to eliminate potential problems in connection with the payment of life insurance benefits where the death is a result of withholding medical treatment, and death occurs within the period specified in the suicide clause contained in all life insurance policies, the statute provides that following the directions contained in the declaration does not constitute suicide or homicide. In addition, the existence of the declaration does not in any way impair any life insurance contract, or justify any increase in a life insurance premium as a result of the existence of the declaration.

CPR Directives

A statement of intent regarding cardiopulmonary resuscitation (CPR) is different from a living will. CPR includes such things as chest compression, delivering electric shock to the chest, or placing tubes in the airway to assist breathing. A CPR Directive is a form that can be obtained only from a physician, and requires the signature of the patient's physician.

Anatomical Gifts

Colorado has enacted the Uniform Anatomical Gifts Act, which governs the donation of organs and tissue at death. The donation may be made to a specified donee, or without specifying a donee. The gift can be made by a person's will, but this is not recommended, since the will may not be discovered until it is too late to carry out the donor's intention.

The donation may also be indicated on an identification card designed to be carried on the person, which is signed by the donor. Delivery during lifetime is not necessary for this form of donation to be effective. However, the donor, or the donor's agent, should notify the federally designated organ procurement agency of the gift, for the purpose of adding the donor's name to the organ and tissue donor registry.

The most common method of indicating the intention to donate organs is to note this on the person's driver's license. A "Y" is placed in the donor field on the front of the license. The Colorado Department of Transportation then electronically transfers the information to the federally designated organ procurement agency.

In the absence of an individual declaration to donate all or part of a person's own body, and if there is no contrary indication by the deceased person, a spouse, or other statutorily designated persons, may make a donation.

Health Care Powers of Attorney

Under the Colorado Patient Autonomy Act, any adult person may designate another adult person as his agent for the purpose of making medical decisions. (See Chapter 20 for additional information regarding powers of attorney.) Upon being admitted to a hospital, there is a requirement that the admissions counselor determine the existence of a living will and a medical durable power of attorney. Copies of these documents will often be placed in the patient's medical records..

If a patient is in a coma, or is otherwise unable to make medical decisions, the agent named in the medical power of attorney is required to act in signing hospital consents and other medical orders, in accordance with the specific terms contained in the power of attorney. If there are no specific directions describing the intention of the patient with regard to the required medical decision, the agent shall act in accordance with the best interests of the patient as determined by the agent.

Proxy Medical Decisions

The Colorado legislature has concluded that the lack of decisional capacity to provide informed consent to or refusal of medical treatment should not preclude such decisions from being made on behalf of a person who has no known advance medical directive, and whose wishes are not otherwise known. The Colorado Patient Autonomy Act allows a health care provider, or health care facility, to rely, in good faith, upon the medical treatment decision of a proxy decision-maker.

The attending physician must make reasonable efforts to locate as many interested persons as practicable, and rely on those persons to notify other interested persons. Interested persons are defined as the patient's spouse, either parent, any adult child, sibling, or grandchild of the patient, or any close friend. The interested persons must then reach a consensus as to who among them shall make medical treatment decisions on behalf of the patient. The person chosen should have a close relationship with the patient, and be the person most likely to be currently informed of the patient's wishes. If the interested persons are unable to agree who should be the proxy decision-maker, then any one of the interested persons may seek to have a court guardianship commenced.

Summary

Individuals who are concerned about the issue of the right to die now have express statutory permission under Colorado law to determine to what extent medical treatment will be extended under terminal conditions. Although most states have enacted legislation, there may still be some states which do not have legislation of this type. A "living will" executed in Colorado might not be valid in a state which does not have the same or similar legislation. In addition to the living will, Colorado has a number of other methods to provide for the continuation of medical care in the event of a disabling medical condition. Because of the sensitivity and importance of this matter, individuals desiring to take advantage of the Colorado law should consult with legal counsel to make certain that the declarations which they prepare are valid, and will be observed at the appropriate time.

SHOULD I HAVE A
PRENUPTIAL AGREEMENT?

*I am a marvelous housekeeper. Every time I leave
a man,
I keep his house.*

— Zsa Zsa Gabor

One of the most hotly discussed issues confronting a couple about to marry, except possibly the suitable size of the diamond ring and the cost of the wedding, is the subject of marital property rights. This is especially true where one of the future spouses has already accumulated a much larger estate that the other. A favorite breeding ground for marital property agreements is the not uncommon situation where Big Daddy, the successfully wealthy business tycoon, does not trust intentions of the bum he sees drooling over his young daughter. With the unfortunate state of marriages in the United States, and the expectation that only a half of them will survive, such concerns are not unreasonable. What happens if you get married without a prenuptial agreement? It depends on whether you get divorced or die.

First, let's look at divorce. The division of property in case of divorce, or legal separation, requires the identification of what

Colorado law refers to as the "marital property" of the parties. In the simplest terms, a person's "separate property" is any property acquired by that person prior to the marriage, and any property acquired by gift or inheritance. Property acquired after the marriage, as well as the increase in the value of separate property, is marital property.

In a divorce proceeding, Colorado law states that marital property is divided by the court in such proportions as the court deems just, after considering all relevant factors. However, in most cases, this means that the marital property is divided about equally. Of course, a person's separate property remains that person's property, and is not subject to division. When couples begin to commingle their assets after marriage, it may create problems years later in trying to identify what is marital property, and what is separate property. Dividing the assets is something divorce lawyers love to do, and they not only enjoy the work, but they also get paid a lot to do it. The rules just stated are very general, and are only intended to give a basic overview of how things work at the time of divorce.

After considering the trauma of dividing assets during a divorce proceeding, some may be inclined to think it would be better to die. But the loss of assets to an unhappy spouse may be even greater at death, than as the result of a divorce. You may want to review the discussion of the rights of a surviving spouse in Chapter 11. Regardless of any last will and testament to the contrary, a surviving spouse may elect to receive a portion of the estate. This is referred to as the "elective share." The amount that may be taken is determined by a vesting schedule, and the schedule rewards the spouse for hanging in there, since the elective share increases with each year the couple is married. If the couple is married for less than a year, the surviving spouse may take only $50,000. Thereafter, the spouse may take 5% of something called the "augmented estate" for each year of marriage, with a maximum of 50% after 10 years of marriage. This election is not limited to the marital property, but includes all property owned by the deceased spouse, subject to some adjustments too technical to discuss in a book of this type.

It is these types of issues that make the subject of prenuptial agreements so engaging. As important as such agreements are in protecting the wealth of the rich bride or groom to be, they also create great controversy between couples about to marry. The economic issues become clouded with issues of trust, and love, and other mushy sentiments. As a result, the subject is often not raised until the wedding is right around the corner, and when it raises its ugly head at this most inopportune moment, the result can be disastrous. For example, there is the groom who was fearful of raising the issue until he and the bride were in the church vestibule signing the marriage certificate, prior to walking down the aisle. He slyly put the antenuptial agreement next to the marriage certificate. The bride, not as starry eyed as the groom had hoped, upon seeing this deceitful ploy, ran crying from the church, leaving the embarrassed groom to explain to the assembled crowd that the wedding would have to wait for another day.

Assuming both parties agree that a prenuptial agreement is important, a significant argument for marrying someone who has as much wealth as you do, it is obviously important that the agreement be valid in case things fall apart after the bloom is off the rose. The Colorado Marital Agreement Act defines what constitutes a legally enforceable prenuptial agreement. In fact, if a couple simply cannot face the prospect of signing such an agreement before the ceremony, or if they forget this important detail in the hectic rush of things, Colorado even allows them to enter into a "postnuptial" agreement after the marriage.

Under the statute, a "marital agreement" is defined as an agreement either between prospective spouses made in contemplation of marriage, or between present spouses, but only if signed by both parties prior to the filing of an action for dissolution of marriage, or for legal separation. The agreement must be signed voluntarily — no twisting of the arm. In addition, each party must make a fair and reasonable disclosure of their property or financial obligations — you can't give it up if you don't know what it is. Although the statute does not require both parties to be represented by a separate lawyer, this is generally agreed as vital to the future enforcement of the contract. No lawyer would represent both parties to such an agreement, since it would be a clear conflict of interest. The initial draft of such an agreement is often just the opening salvo in an extended negotiation, which eventually results in rights and obligations both parties can tolerate. These agreements are complicated and technical, and should not be entrusted to the lawyer who fixes your traffic tickets.

Remember the Zsa Zsa quote at the beginning of this chapter, and let me recount a personal experience which demonstrates the importance of following the rules. A wealthy retired physician came to me for estate planning advice. He had been divorced, and later remarried a lovely lady forty years his junior. Understanding that his muscular physique may not have been the most interesting aspect of the relationship, he insisted on, and received, a prenuptial agreement to protect his estate. Upon inquiry, it was determined that the lovely lady had not seen a financial statement, and had not been advised to consult with an attorney of her own choosing prior to signing the agreement. With great reluctance, I informed the good doctor that it was very probable the agreement would not stand up in a court of law, but reminded him of the possibility of curing the problem with a postnuptial agreement. My client opined that would be no problem. His new wife was willing to sign a postnuptial agreement, but now sought the advice of an attorney. The result is that she signed the agreement, but only after receiving a check in the amount of $100,000 from the perplexed physician's retirement account, and the promise of an insurance policy for $1,000,000 on his life.

Need I say more?

Summary

The subject of marital property agreements is very sensitive, especially to couples anticipating entering into a "lifelong" relationship of marital bliss. Only those more experienced in marital relationships and the stresses of modern life realize that the road to happiness in marriage is often filled with many potholes. Where there is substantial wealth owned by one of the prospective marital partners, especially when such wealth in inherited, or where there has been a previous marriage with children, the importance of having an understanding regarding the disposition of wealth in the event of divorce or death will reduce the possibility of future conflicts.

ASSET PROTECTION[1]

*When the mouse laughs at the rat, there's a hole
   nearby.*

— Nigerian Proverb

What Is Asset Protection?

Perhaps we should first discuss what asset protection is not. If you look in the Attorney listings in the Denver Yellow Pages, you will not (as of January 2003) find a category for "Asset Protection." There are a number of people marketing asset protection seminars. They give free or very low cost seminars at which they try to scare you over the "litigation explosion," and then tell you that the way to protect yourself is to buy their package of limited partnership and trust documents for $2,000 or more. Don't buy this stuff. Limited partnerships and trusts are good tools for many purposes. However, often the limited partnership documents and trust documents being sold by these marketers are not only inappropriate for the purchaser's situation, they are not drafted properly to work right in an

[1] This chapter was contributed by Denver attorney Allen Sparkman with the firm of Sparkman, Shaffer, Perlick LLP at 600 17th Street, Suite 2800 South, Denver, CO 80202. 303-449-6543. sparkman@sspattorneys.com. Mr. Sparkman's practice emphasizes estate planning and asset protection law.

appropriate situation. Don't believe sales people who tell you that they've figured out a way that you can run all your earnings through a multileveled foreign structure and avoid United States income taxes.

People work hard to accumulate wealth, and they want to preserve their wealth for their retirement and for their heirs. Many events may threaten the wealth that an individual has amassed. Accidents, illness, divorce, bad business results, natural disasters – all these and more endanger financial well-being. Asset protection may be thought of as a form of risk management.

The Starting Point

For most people, the starting point in risk management, or asset protection, is reviewing their insurance to make sure that coverage is adequate. You should consider all the things that you would need, or want badly, to replace in the event all your possessions were destroyed. Consider if your home has appreciated substantially; is the insurance you took out when you purchased it still adequate? Do you have adequate automobile insurance, property and casualty insurance, health insurance, major medical, disability and long-term care insurance?

What of possible accidents that you may cause, such as an auto accident? Do not assume you are fine so long as you have the statutory minimum coverages. An accident might cause much greater damages than would be covered by the statutory minimums, and if you, or another driver for whom you have responsibility, cause an accident, you may be sued for damages over and above your insurance coverage. Even if you do not own property now that you are worried about losing, remember that a judgment taken against you will be good for 20 years, and may be renewed if it is not satisfied in that time. Thus, someone who is severely injured may wait around until you are well established in a career and then seek to collect for a judgment arising from an accident many years ago.

If you have very large cash balances (over $100,000) in bank accounts, make sure that you have arranged the accounts to achieve the most deposit insurance you can. A booklet explaining the various arrangements that can improve your deposit coverage is available from the Federal Deposit Insurance Commission or at www.fdic.gov/deposits/insured/index.html.

Exempt Property

If you've taken care of the basic, that is you have adequate insurance and you lead a careful lifestyle, what will happen if disaster does strike and all your assets are in peril of being taken to satisfy a creditor? Colorado, like all states, provides that certain property is exempt from the claims of creditors. You may have read of some states that provide an exemption for an individual's homestead, no matter how valuable. Colorado is not one of those states. Only $45,000 of the equity in a person's homestead is exempt under Colorado law. Colorado does provide unlimited exemptions for benefits held in retirement plans (including IRAs) (except for judgments for arrearages in child support), and for the proceeds of life insurance paid at the death of the debtor, unless the life insurance is payable to the debtor's estate. Life insurance proceeds are not exempt, however, from claims of creditors of the beneficiary who receives the proceeds. This is one reason that people who want to make sure that the insurance on their lives will benefit their family will arrange for the insurance to be owned by an irrevocable life insurance trust. As discussed below, the proper use of trusts is a very useful tool in asset protection planning.

With regard to the exemption for up to $45,000 of the value of a homestead, people should be aware that most mortgages provide for a waiver of the homestead exemption as to the mortgage debt, and that the Colorado homestead exemption is not available against a federal tax lien. If any other judgment creditor wants to levy on the debtor's homestead, the creditor must file an affidavit stating that the appraised value of the homestead exceeds the liens against the homestead, including the lien of the judgment creditor.

Other exemptions under Colorado law protect a portion of the cash value of life insurance on the debtor's life, modest amounts of household furnishings jewelry, apparel, tools, equipment or books used in a business or profession, and other items.

The Internal Revenue Code specifies what property is exempt from levy to satisfy a lien for federal taxes. The list of property exempt for this purpose differs from the property that is exempt under Colorado law. It includes a small amount for wages, but, depending on the circumstances, the taxpayer's principal residence and business property may be exempt from a federal tax levy.

Fraudulent Transfers

If you want to do some planning to try to protect more of your assets, you must consider the Colorado Uniform Fraudulent Transfer Act (referred to as "CUFTA"). CUFTA exists to prevent debtors from transferring their assets out of the reach of their creditors, and is based on law that first developed in England over four hundred years ago during the reign of Elizabeth I. Many people might agree that it would be wrong, for example, if someone who has just injured another person in an accident could transfer all of his assets to a spouse, or child, and thus frustrate the ability of the injured person to be compensated through an award of damages. Likewise, many would agree that a spouse, just before a divorce, should not be permitted to impoverish the other spouse and the children by transferring assets to, say, a trust organized under the laws of a foreign jurisdiction. Although perhaps with more sympathy for the debtor, most would also agree that a taxpayer should not be able to prevent collection of taxes justly owed by transfers of the taxpayer's assets out of the reach of the tax collector.

CUFTA's reach is much broader than these cases on which we might all agree. CUFTA treats as fraudulent any transfer made, or obligation incurred, by a debtor if the transfer was made, or the obligation incurred, with actual intent to hinder, delay, or defraud any present or future creditor of the debtor. In this situation, "fraudulent" does not mean criminal or tortuous fraud, but only that the transfer, or obligation, is not valid as to creditors, and may be set aside so that the asset will be available to satisfy the creditor's claim. In addition to transfers made, or obligations incurred, with actual intent to impede a creditor, CUFTA reaches many more situations. If a debtor makes a gift to the debtor's children, for example, the gift may be set aside under CUFTA if the debtor was engaged or was about to engage in a business or a transaction for which the remaining assets of the debtor were unreasonably small in relation to the business or transaction the debtor intended to incur. A gift may also be set aside under CUFTA if the debtor believed, or reasonably should have believed, that he would incur debts beyond the debtor's ability to pay as they became due. Also, in the case of a gift or a transaction that is partly a gift, a transfer made, or obligation incurred, by a debtor is fraudulent as to a creditor whose claim arose before the transfer was made, or the obligation was incurred, if the debtor was insolvent at that time, or the debtor became insolvent as a result of the transfer or obligation. As to existing creditors, CUFTA also characterizes a transfer as fraudulent: (i) if the transfer was made to an insider of the debtor (such as a family member or business partner) for an antecedent debt, (ii) the debtor was insolvent at that time, and (iii) the insider had reasonable cause to believe that the debtor was insolvent. Be aware that solvency under CUFTA is computed by ignoring exempt assets in the calculation. Therefore, if you want to know if you are solvent for purposes of CUFTA, you should have your balance sheet reviewed by an advisor who is knowledgeable about CUFTA.

To determine if a debtor transferred property or incurred an obligation with actual intent to impede any creditor, CUFTA specifies several factors that may be considered:

- Was the transfer or obligation to an insider?
- Did the debtor retain possession or control of the property transferred after the transfer?

- Was the transfer or obligation disclosed or concealed?
- Before the transfer was made or obligation was incurred, had the debtor been sued or threatened with suit?
- Was the transfer of substantially all the debtor's assets?
- Did the debtor abscond?
- Did the debtor remove or conceal assets?
- Was the value of the consideration received by the debtor reasonably equivalent to the value of the asset transferred or the amount of the obligation incurred?
- Was the debtor insolvent or become insolvent shortly after the transfer was made or the obligation was incurred?
- Did the transfer occur shortly before or shortly after a substantial debt was incurred?
- Did the debtor transfer the essential assets of the business to a lienor who transferred the assets to an insider of the debtor?

This is not an exclusive list of factors that a court may consider.

When a creditor sues a debtor, the creditor may join in the same lawsuit any transferee of the debtor, if the creditor wants to claim that a transfer by the debtor to the transferee was fraudulent as to the creditor.

An Approach to Asset Protection Planning

If you are solvent and you wish to take steps to enhance the safety of your assets against obligations that may arise in the future, you should be aware that no method of attempting to protect assets from creditors is totally fool-proof, and no one method should be used singly. Proper, effective asset protection planning requires a multidisciplinary approach that, depending upon your individual situation, may require advice from insurance advisors, tax and estate planning advisors, business advisors, litigation attorneys, and others. An effective asset protection arrangement will be based on layers of protection.

Techniques that might be used include the following:

- Marital/premarital agreements

- Increasing the portion of your assets that are in exempt categories; for example, increasing the amount you contribute to a 401(k) plan or IRA
- Transferring assets to a limited partnership or limited liability company
- Conducting your business in the most tax-efficient, and most asset-protective, form
- Gifting or selling assets to family members (or to trusts for their benefit)
- Transferring assets to trusts

Marital/Premarital Agreements

Written marital and premarital agreements allow spouses to provide for how property is to be treated in the event of divorce, or in the event of the death of either spouse. For example, one spouse can waive his right to elect against the estate of the other spouse, and the spouses can provide that gifts from one to the other will be considered the separate property of the donee.

Increasing the Amount of Exempt Assets

If you are able to do so, consider selling assets and using the cash to acquire exempt assets such as a homestead (if you do not already have one), or beginning or adding to a retirement program. Courts have held that such transfers before filing for bankruptcy do not create a voidable preference, but it is uncertain how they might be treated under CUFTA.

Transferring Assets to Limited Partnerships or Limited Liability Companies

If a debtor owns an asset outright, such as land held for investment, or stock in a corporation, a judgment creditor can execute on that asset and cause it to be sold. In the case of corporate stock, a creditor might be able to gain control of the stock, and thus, the corporation. If assets are held by a limited partnership or limited liability company, however, Colorado law (and the law of every state, to one degree or another) provides that a judgment creditor of a partner or member cannot levy on the assets of the entity, or on the partnership or membership interest of the debtor. Instead, the judgment creditor may only obtain what is known as a "charging order." A charging order directs the limited partnership or limited liability company to pay whatever it would have paid to the debtor to the judgment creditor instead. Often the amount or timing of payments under a charging order will be very uncertain. If the judgment creditor can convince a court to allow foreclosure on the partnership or membership interest, the judgment creditor will likely only become an assignee of the interest, and will not obtain any management rights with respect to the entity. The judgment creditor may be subject to unfavorable income tax consequences by being taxed on income of the entity, even if that income is not actually paid to the creditor. The asset protection features of a limited partnership or limited liability company are enhanced if the debtor is not in control of the entity.

Conducting Your Business in the Most Tax-Efficient and Asset-Protective Form

Colorado law permits a limited liability company to be organized with only one member. Many attorneys question whether a single-member LLC will provide any asset protection because the policy reasons for only allowing charging orders do not seem to apply when there is only one member. That is, there are no other owners whose assets will be unfairly impacted, and allowing levy on the assets of the LLC would not depress the value of the LLC to the detriment of owners other than the debtor or of the creditor.

Also, no entity will protect an individual against his own negligence. For example, if a person designs and manufactures custom furniture without the assistance of any employees or contractors, any injuries resulting from faulty design or manufacture will be the result of that person's actions, and it will not matter if the business is conducted as a sole proprietorship, a corporation, a limited partnership, or a limited liability company. With respect to an individual's own negligence, insurance should be used to protect against liability.

If you conduct a business with employees or partners, you should consider forming a corporation, partnership, or limited liability company to conduct the business, and to protect yourself against liability for the acts of your employees or partners. Partnerships, limited liability companies, and S corporations will provide one level of income taxation. In some cases, an S corporation will be the preferred choice because of the potential for saving on employment taxes. This advantage must be balanced against the more favorable asset protection features of limited partnerships and limited liability companies that are discussed above in this chapter. Professionals, such as attorneys and physicians, must be particularly careful to comply with rules of their profession governing practice through an entity. If you have questions concerning how your business should be conducted, consulted a qualified advisor.

Gifting or Selling Assets to Family Members

A person may own real estate, for example, that they would like to keep in their family and protect from possible creditors. One way to do this might be to transfer the real estate to a limited partnership or limited liability company, and then gift interests in the entity to family members, or to a trust for their benefit. However, gifts in many situations are subject to challenge as being fraudulent under CUFTA. If an asset is sold for fair market value to family members, or to a trust for their benefit, the sale may be challenged under CUFTA only if a creditor can show that the sale was carried out with actual intent to defraud the creditor. The sale may be made for a long-term unsecured note that pays only interest for a number of years. The terms of the note, and other terms of the sale, such as down payment, must be such that the debtor will be considered to have received fair market value for the property. If the sale is not for fair market value, the sale will be subject to attack under CUFTA as a gift, and certain tax benefits will be lost as well. After the sale, the debtor owns the promissory note, and the note will be subject to execution by a judgment creditor. However, the terms of the note will make it much less attractive to a creditor than the sold property would have been.

Transfers to Trusts

Many trust marketers and seminar marketers give the impression that a revocable living trust provides tax benefits or asset protection features. Neither is true. Because a revocable living trust is, by its nature, revocable at any time by the grantor, it does not provide any asset protection to the grantor. A revocable living trust provides certain benefits, such as avoiding probate, and providing privacy for the grantor's testamentary gifts. Although probate in Colorado is a relatively simple and straightforward process, a person's survivors may appreciate it if assets have been transferred before death to the grantor's revocable living trust so that paperwork and other details are lessened after death. Also, if a Colorado resident owns real estate in another state, steps should be taken to convey title to such real estate into the name of the trust. Transferring title to the out-of-state real estate to a revocable living trust will avoid ancillary probate.

What about transferring assets to an irrevocable trust? If the grantor is to be a beneficiary of the trust, the laws of most states provide that the transfer to the trust will not insulate the transferred assets from the reach of the grantor's creditors. It is possible that the Colorado law in this regard applies only to creditors who exist at the time of the transfer to the trust. Some states, such as Alaska, Delaware, and Nevada, have passed statutes to allow trusts that benefit the grantor and that are also protected from the grantor's creditors. These statutes are all new. No cases have been decided under them. The assets to be protected must be held by a trustee residing in one of these states. The grantor loses control of the assets.

Many asset protection plans are based on the transfer of assets to a foreign trust. Under this approach, the client transfers assets to a trust organized under the laws of a foreign jurisdiction. Several factors guide the choice of jurisdiction, the most important of which is that the foreign jurisdiction does not recognize judgments of foreign courts. If the foreign jurisdiction would not recognize the judgment of a Colorado court, a creditor, who wanted to pursue a debtor who had transferred assets to the foreign trust, would have to sue in the foreign jurisdiction. The foreign jurisdiction will likely have very stringent proof requirements for the creditor to meet, and bank secrecy laws will impede the creditor's learning details of the trust arrangement. The creditor in this scenario faces an entirely different, and much more difficult, situation than the creditor pursuing a debtor who has established a trust under the laws of Colorado. Because of the federal constitution's full faith and credit clause, a creditor who obtains a judgment against a debtor in a Colorado court does not have to relitigate the liability issues in the other state, but can simply sue on the judgment obtained in Colorado.

Someone who is curious about whether a foreign trust is right for himself should consider at least the following:

- Setting up a foreign trust arrangement properly is expensive. The fees and expenses of lawyers and other advisors, including the foreign trustee, may run to several thousands of dollars.
- Timing is vital. If a debtor transfers substantially all of his assets to a foreign trust shortly before, or after, incurring a major obligation, the debtor may be facing civil contempt charges in a United States court if the debtor refuses to bring the assets back.

Trusts for Beneficiaries Other than the Grantor

It is much easier to provide asset protection to family members when gifts or bequests are made to them, than it is for an individual to protect his own assets. If a parent makes gifts or bequests outright to a child, the assets then become subject to claims of the child's creditors. If, instead, the parent makes the gift or bequest to a trust for the child's benefit, and if the trust document limits the child's benefits under the trust, a creditor of the beneficiary will find it very hard to reach assets of the trust. Also, if the child goes through a divorce, the assets in the trust may be fully or partially protected. Gifting assets in trust also provides protection against importuning by the child's spouse for investment in the spouse's business venture, and against other problems the child may encounter, such as substance abuse. A trust cannot achieve these benefits unless it is properly drafted.

The assets that will be transferred to a trust often will be interests in a limited partnership or limited liability company. Often, an individual who owns multiple parcels of real estate will form a separate limited liability company for each parcel, and will form a management limited liability company to own interests in all the other LLCs. Interests in the management LLC will then be contributed, or sold, to a trust for the benefit of the individual's family. To be successful, a creditor will have to get past the trust, the management LLC, and then an individual real estate LLC to be able to get at any of the real estate. This is one example of layering in asset protection.

Summary

Asset protection is a form of risk management. The starting point for any effective program of risk management is adequate insurance. Beyond insurance, there are many techniques available to help insulate assets from creditors. Picking the right technique, or techniques, to use in a particular setting requires advisors who understand the individual's situation, goals, fears and desires, and who understand CUFTA and the relevant tax, estate planning, business, and debtor-creditor legal issues.

LONG-TERM CARE AND MEDICAID PLANNING[2]

The future must be shaped or it will impose itself as catastrophe.

— Henry A. Kissinger

Introduction

Long-term care planning is an important part of estate planning, and unfortunately it is often overlooked. There are many reasons that planning for long-term care is overlooked. Often this oversight involves issues beyond simple economics.

Most people do not like to face their own mortality and feel that they will never need long-term care. However, in reality, according to a study published by the *New England Journal of Medicine*, almost half of all Americans will spend some time in a nursing home. Therefore, most couples will likely have to deal with long-term care planning for one spouse. This also means that a large

[2] This chapter was contributed by Denver attorneys Joseph A. Dawson and Marco D. Chayet, partners with the firm of Chayet, Young & Dawson, LLC, at 425 Cherry Street, Suite 350, Denver, CO 80246. 303-355-8500. contact@cydlaw.com. They are elder law attorneys who concentrate on designing and implementing complex estate plans, including long-term care planning and Medicaid planning.

majority of Colorado families will have to deal with some type of long-term care issues for one, or possibly both, parents.

Even if an individual acknowledges the possibility of needing long-term care, they still may not understand how expensive this type of care can be. The average cost of nursing home care in Colorado in 2003 is approximately $4,500 per month, and in some areas of the United States this average cost exceeds $10,000 per month. Given these figures, an individual could spend as much as $300,000 to $400,000 on long-term care in his lifetime. It is often the case that a married couple can have their entire life savings wiped out by one spouse's long-term care needs in just a few years.

What Is Long-Term Care?

The type of health care most individuals require can be divided into two categories: skilled care and custodial care.

Skilled care is the type of care that is provided by health care professionals, such as doctors, nurses, or therapists. Skilled care is generally administered in a hospital, a doctor's office, or a rehabilitation facility. Skilled care can also be administered at home, in an assisted living facility, or in a nursing home. This type of care is normally paid for by an individual's private health insurance, the Medicare program, and possibly a supplemental or "Medi-gap" type policy.

Custodial care is the type of care that provides assistance with activities of daily living, such as general supervision to prevent physical harm, or to assist with bathing, toileting, transitioning, dressing, etc. This type of care can be required due to an individual's physical needs, or some mental deficiency, such as dementia brought on by injury or age. Custodial care is generally administered in the home, an assisted living facility, or a nursing home. These long-term care costs are typically not covered by private insurance, Medicare, or Medi-gap policies.

How to Pay for Long-Term Care?

There are four ways to pay for custodial or long-term care: (1) Veterans benefits, (2) long-term care insurance, (3) private payments, and (4) Medicaid. Less than 1% of nursing home residents are receiving Veterans benefits. Only about 5% to 8% of Americans have long-term care insurance. Many individuals who necessitate long-term care are uninsurable due to age and health problems. If you can afford long-term care insurance and are insurable, you should investigate the purchase of a long-term care policy as part of your long-term care planning. If not, you will have to consider other options.

Since a very small portion of the population owns long-term care insurance and an even smaller portion receive benefits, such as Veterans benefits, the two options that pay for the majority of long-term care in Colorado are private payments and Medicaid. As discussed above, private payments for long-term care are extremely expensive. In order to plan on private payments for long-term care, you will need to consult with a financial planner familiar with long-term care issues to formulate a sound financial plan for privately paying for your long-term care. If you can afford to accomplish this type of planning, you should do so early. It will take time to implement a private pay plan and even more time to allow your plan and its investments to grow.

Few people can afford to privately pay for long-term care, and some who might have been able to afford private payment have failed to adequately plan for that circumstance. Thus, Medicaid, by default, is the majority payer of long-term care costs in most states. For this reason, Medicaid planning can be an important component to most individuals' long-term care planning.

Medicaid Planning as a Long-Term Care Option

Medicaid planning is the planning required to preserve assets, and prevent estate recovery, while obtaining Medicaid eligibility in a timely manner. Medicaid is a need-based program and, although partially funded by the federal government and mandated by federal regulations, it is run by each individual state at the county level. This means that each state, including Colorado, has its own Medicaid regulations that comply with the federally mandated Medicaid laws. The entity administrating Medicaid in Colorado is the Colorado Department of Health Care Policy and Financing (CDHPF). The majority of people on Medicaid are receiving long-term care in a facility, such as an assisted living facility or nursing home. However, through Medicaid's Home and Community Based Services (HCBS) waiver program, individuals can also receive limited custodial care in the home.

Since Medicaid is a need-based program, an applicant will have to meet certain financial and medical need-based limits. There are three basic "tests" each applicant must meet to become Medicaid eligible: (1) the medical test, (2) the income test, and (3) the asset test.

Medical Test

The medical test establishes that the applicant requires the type of custodial care covered by the Medicaid program. This is done by an assessment from the applicant's doctor or other professional health care provider. The applicant's doctor or health care provider will evaluate the applicant's need for assistance with daily activities, and report these needs to the state agency that provides for Medicaid coverage. In Colorado, the local agency responsible for administering Medicaid is the respective county department of human services. If the applicant is currently receiving care in a facility, such as a nursing home, then this assessment is usually fairly easy to complete. If the applicant is applying for one of Medicaid's waiver programs to receive in-home care, an assessment may also need to be done.

Income Test

In Colorado, for the year 2003, the applicant's allowable monthly income for Medicaid eligibility is $1,656. Technically, the applicant cannot make more than $1,656 a month and still become eligible for Medicaid. However, if the applicant has income above the $1,656 limit, but below the average cost of nursing home care in his region, then the applicant can still become eligible for Medicaid by setting up a special trust for the excess income known as an income trust or a "Utah gap" trust. The trust is established to hold the income over the $1,656 cap but below the regional income cap. This amount will still be attributed to the applicant's long-term care cost, either in the form of a monthly payment to the nursing home, or a monthly income allowance to the community spouse (the healthy spouse still living in the community). Any funds remaining in the income trust account upon the applicant's death or termination from the Medicaid program will go back to the state in the form of a repayment for any long-term care cost the state has paid for the individual.

For the purpose of determining the average cost of nursing home care in certain areas, known as the regional cap, Colorado is split into four regions. These regions are divided by counties. For example, Region I is comprised of Adams, Arapahoe, Boulder, Denver, and Jefferson counties and has an average nursing home cost of $4,747. The other three regions (Regions II, III, IV) are made up of the remaining outlying counties.

For married couples, the income test becomes even more complicated. Along with the possibility of an income trust, the community spouse may be eligible for an amount attributed back to them from the institutionalized spouse's income. This amount would be to help pay for a Minimum Monthly Maintenance Needs Allowance (MMMNA). If the community spouse does not have enough income to pay for this MMMNA, then a portion of the institutionalized spouse's income will be attributed back to the community spouse. This payment from the institutionalized spouse back to the community spouse is known as the Monthly Income Allowance (MIA).

If a married couple or family finds themselves involved in the Medicaid program to the extent that they are required to establish an income trust, or calculate Minimum Monthly Maintenance Needs

Allowances or Monthly Income Allowances, they should seek the advice of an elder law attorney competent in Medicaid planning. Such an attorney can ensure that the community spouse is receiving all post-eligibility income allowances he is entitled to receive under current Medicaid regulations.

Asset Test

Unmarried applicants cannot have more than $2,000 in countable assets to become Medicaid eligible. A countable asset is an asset that is not considered exempt under one of the current Medicaid exemption regulations. Below are examples of the most common exemptions that are not considered countable assets:

(1) Primary Residence

The primary residence of the applicant is not considered a countable asset if it was the applicant's primary residence, and the applicant (or spouse) actually lived in the home immediately prior to being institutionalized. To insure that the home remains an exempt asset, the applicant should have the intent to return home, or the spouse or a dependent relative should continue to live there. This residential exemption also applies to mobile homes used as the principal residence, and any other outlying structures, such as garages or sheds.

(2) Vehicles

The applicant is allowed one vehicle as an exemption, as long as its market value is $4,500 or less. However, this $4,500 dollar limitation is eliminated if the car is used for transportation to employment, or to obtain medical treatment. In addition, the vehicle will be exempt if it is specially equipped for a disabled applicant, or is required due to terrain or distance. In Colorado, the applicant must obtain a letter from a physician or employer to establish the vehicle's exempt status. Finally, there is no limit on the value of one vehicle owned by a married couple.

(3) Personal Property

The applicant's personal property is exempt up to a total value of $2,000. This amount does not include certain exempt personal items, such as wedding and engagement rings of any value. Again, this personal property limit is does not apply to married couples.

(4) Life Insurance

The applicant is allowed to retain certain life insurance policies, as long as the total face value of all policies does not exceed $1,500. If the face value is more than $1,500, the policy is exempt only if the cash value is below the $1,500 cap. In cases where the cash value does exceed $1,500, the applicant will have to cash out the policy and spend down the proceeds before the applicant can become Medicaid eligible. Term life insurance policies are excluded from this calculation.

(5) Burial Insurance

Certain types of burial insurance are also exempt. Irrevocable burial plans are exempt regardless of their dollar value. However, if a burial policy is revocable, then the burial insurance is exempt to a maximum of $1,500. Revocable insurance allows you or a family member to receive back any funds not spent on the burial. Irrevocable insurance will not allow for any payment of unused portions, even if the funds are not completely spent on the burial. Other burial expenses, and items that are exempt, include the value of burial spaces and grave markers for the applicant and immediate family members.

(6) Community Spouse Resource Allowance

In addition to the exemptions mentioned above, the community spouse, that is the well spouse living in the community, is allowed an additional exemption. The community spouse is allowed to retain a Community Spouse Resource Allowance (CSRA). The CSRA is in addition to amount of assets over the normal $2,000 limit for the institutionalized spouse. The CSRA for 2003 is $90,660. Medicaid's determination of the CSRA is adjusted yearly based on different factors such as inflation.

Medicaid Regulations Involving Complex Assets

In addition to the many regulations regarding the above mentioned exemptions, Medicaid also has a variety of rules dealing with other complex assets such as annuities, trusts, promissory notes, reverse mortgages, life estates, IRAs, and retirement accounts. The Medicaid regulations regarding these special assets have become very complex and would require a much more extensive description than can be provided in this chapter. Again, please consult a competent Medicaid attorney if you have specific questions regarding these complex assets.

Issues Regarding the Home and Estate Recovery

The State of Colorado, through its Medical Assistance Estate Recovery Program, can seek recovery for the amount of medical assistance provided to an individual once that individual has died, or is no longer eligible for the Medicaid program. Therefore, the state can be an interested party in the administration and settlement of a Medicaid recipient's estate.

When a Medicaid recipient dies, the state must be notified of the death, and be given notice of the individual's estate proceedings. The state will then try to assert a lien against the individual's estate to obtain reimbursement for the assistance it provided. In an effort to be reimbursed for the monies the state spent on behalf of the Medicaid applicant, the state will file a claim against the individual's estate. The claim can attach to the equity in the home, or attach to whatever assets may be in the estate of the deceased Medicaid applicant. The amount of the recovery is based on a dollar-for-dollar lien against the Medicaid applicant's estate, but the state can only recover to the limits of what is contained in the Medicaid applicant's estate. The state cannot recover against any other persons that may jointly own property within the estate. For example, if an individual dies after receiving Medicaid, and he still owned a residence at the time of death, the state is going to place a lien on the residence to recoup its portion of the long-term care payments in a dollar-for-dollar amount.

Due to the possibility of estate recovery liens, it is essential that anyone initiating Medicaid planning incorporate into their plans a method of recovery prevention. This can be done in a variety of ways, but one general concept may be to retitle the primary residence in such a way as to prevent estate recovery when the Medicaid recipient dies. A competent Medicaid attorney should be consulted before doing any retitling of assets.

The Look-Back Period and Ineligibility Periods

In the past, Medicaid found that individuals were transferring large sums of money to their loved ones before applying for the Medicaid program in an effort to circumvent Medicaid laws. To eliminate this problem, Medicaid implemented ineligibility periods tied to these types of transfers. Although the concept was correct, there was an unintended consequence to these transfer regulations that actually made it easier for attorneys to implement Medicaid planning. When discussing these transfer regulations you should be aware of two different time periods that Medicaid uses to impose ineligibility periods. These two periods are the look-back period, and ineligibility period.

Many people confuse Medicaid's three-year look-back period with the ineligibility period. Clients often assume that because they have made a transfer of assets, they have a three-year penalty period. In fact, the look-back period and ineligibility period are two distinct time frames. In light of the confusion surrounding these different periods, it is instructive to first define them before discussing how they are used in Medicaid planning.

Medicaid is allowed to "look back" three years into an applicant's financial past to determine if he has made any transfers without consideration. For transfers into or out of trusts, the look-back period is five years. A transfer without consideration is basically a gift. When you buy a radio for $100 dollars, you have made a transfer for consideration. You have transferred $100 for the consideration of receiving the radio. A transfer without consideration means you give something without getting anything in return.

If Medicaid determines that an applicant has made a transfer without consideration within the three-year look-back period, they will impose an ineligibility period based on the amount of the transfer and when the transfer was made. It is called an ineligibility period because an individual will be ineligible for Medicaid until the ineligibility period ends. There is no ineligibility period imposed for transfers between spouses. The ineligibility period is calculated by taking the amount of the transfer and dividing that amount by the yearly average cost of nursing home care for the state. The ineligibility period starts from the date of the transfer. The asset transferred does not have to be money. If, for example, an individual transferred a car to a child, Medicaid would claim that the fair market value of the car at the time of the transfer was the amount transferred without consideration.

An example may help to illustrate how these transfer regulations work. Say a father gave his son $60,000 on May 1, 2002. On May 15, 2003, the father applies for Medicaid. Medicaid will then "look back" three years to determine if the father has made any transfers without consideration. Medicaid determines that the $60,000 transfer to the son on May 1, 2002, was a transfer without consideration, and since it falls within the look-back period, they will impose an ineligibility period on the father. To determine the ineligibility period, Medicaid will take the $60,000 transfer amount and divide it by $4,065, which is Medicaid's figure for the average cost of nursing home care in Colorado for the year 2002. When you divide $60,000 by $4,065 you get 14.76. This is the number of months and days of ineligibility incurred by the transfer. This means that the father will be ineligible for Medicaid for 14 months and 23 days. ($60,000 ÷ $4,065 = 14.76; Medicaid regulations state that you take the decimal value and multiply by 30 days to determine how many days of ineligibility are imposed (.76 x 30 days = 22.8 or 23 days). More specifically, the ineligibility period starts at the time of the transfer, May 1, 2002, so the father will be ineligible for Medicaid until August 24, 2003. Since the father applied in May of 2003, his application will be denied and he will have to re-apply after August 24, 2003.

Elder law attorneys now know how Medicaid calculates the ineligibility periods. This means that proper Medicaid planning can use these transfers as a planning tool to preserve a portion of the Medicaid applicant's assets. As part of this type of planning, it is vital that the applicant holds back enough countable assets to privately pay for his expenses and long-term care costs during the ineligibility period. The positive end result is that the people who make these transfers may become Medicaid eligible faster than if they simply spent down their remaining countable assets to the $2,000 countable limit.

The look-back period can also be used as a planning tool. For example, if we wish to make a large gift that would incur an ineligibility period greater than three years, we actually only have to plan on a three year "ineligibility" period because we know that Medicaid can only look back three years to determine if a gift has been made.

Medicaid Planning Techniques

When undertaking Medicaid planning with your attorney, you must first establish your goals. Normally, the goal is to become Medicaid eligible in a timely manner, while preserving as many assets as possible, and preventing any future estate recovery liens. Most individuals' goals will vary depending on their own unique situation. Some individuals may wish to preserve the family home for their children. Others may wish to transfer as many assets as possible to their children as an early inheritance. Still others may not want to make any transfers, and simply become Medicaid eligible as fast as possible by spending down, and building up their exemptions.

Once you have determined you goal, you and your attorney can pick a planning technique that will help you accomplish your goal. As mentioned above, you may wish to use the transfer and hold-back technique. You may also wish to spend down countable assets by paying off debts or purchasing exempt items such as a new car. You can also spend down countable assets by making repairs to your residence, or paying down an existing mortgage, thereby increasing the value of the residence.

Within your planning, you will also want to formulate a time line, incorporating the look-back period, and any potential ineligibility periods, so you know when you will become Medicaid eligible. The time line will also help you determine when to apply for Medicaid, since the application process can take as long as three months to complete.

Finally, you will also want to incorporate into your Medicaid planning a way to prevent any estate recovery liens. This can be done by retitling the property to a spouse, or gifting a portion of the property to a loved one as a joint tenant, or under a life estate. Remember the lien can only attach to the portion of the property that is in the name of the Medicaid recipient. Therefore, if the property is not in the Medicaid recipient's name, or of it will revert to someone else upon their death, then no lien can attach. Keep in mind that if you do retitle the property without consideration to someone other than a spouse, there will be an ineligibility period imposed. This means you will have to plan for this ineligibility period by holding back funds to privately pay for care. In addition, since most residential properties are valued fairly high, the ineligibility period incurred from this type of transfer may be substantial.

Timely Medicaid Planning Is Essential

The time to do Medicaid planning is not when the individual is already in need of custodial care. As you can see from the discussion regarding the look-back period and ineligibility periods, this type of planning takes time. You would ideally like to do Medicaid planning at least three years prior to the need for long-term care. Of course, if an individual is already receiving custodial care and privately paying for that care, Medicaid planning can still be beneficial to reduce the amount of assets that will be consumed by the private payments.

How does an individual or family member know when to begin Medicaid planning? You need to look for signs that an individual will likely need custodial care in the near future. You can look to the individual's medical history, his age, his mental capacity, and whether he is exhibiting signs of dementia, or whether he has received custodial care in the past. There are also other timing issues to consider when doing Medicaid planning. These include whether the individual is willing, or even able, to participate in the Medicaid planning for himself at the time it is required, or whether it is time for a family member to step in and assist with the planning.

Other Issues to Consider in Medicaid Planning

Most Medicaid planning is done for the elderly and, often times, elderly individuals have capacity issues. This means that a large portion of the individuals that require Medicaid planning may lack the mental capacity to initiate, or even assist in, their own Medicaid planning. Therefore, spouses or family members will have to step in to assist the individual in his Medicaid plans. To do this, the family member must have the legal authority to access the individual's financial assets in order to accomplish any transfers or retitling associated with Medicaid planning.

The most common method family members use to access a loved ones's assets is through a Financial Power of Attorney (POA). POA's allow the principal (generally the Medicaid applicant) to appoint an agent to act for him in financial matters. The extent of what the agent can do for the principal is spelled out within the language of the POA. For Medicaid planning purposes, POA's should allow the agent to easily access assets, retitle real property, spend down assets on exemptions, and transfer funds to other individuals, including the agent. Remember that a POA is a very powerful document, and the principal should pick his agent very carefully. The agent should generally be a very responsible family member or friend, or be a reliable third-party institution like a bank.

Some POAs, where the drafter does not envision future Medicaid planning, will limit the agents powers in ways that make Medicaid planning difficult. For example, many Powers of Attorney will limit any gifting to the federal gift tax limit of $11,000. However, for Medicaid planning purposes, most transfers will be greater than this amount.

There are several ways to draft POAs to make them more friendly to Medicaid planning. One way is to not restrict the gifting powers to certain limits, as discussed above. Another is to make sure that the residence, or other real property, is specifically listed within the real property section of the POA, so the agent will be able to sell or retitle the property more easily. The POA should also have successor agents available in case the first choice for an agent is unavailable to do the Medicaid planning.

It is often problematic when an individual who requires Medicaid planning does not have an appropriate POA in place, particularly if the Medicaid applicant has lost his mental capacity to properly execute a POA. If this is the case, then the only other alternative to accessing assets held exclusively by that individual is to petition the Court for a conservatorship. When you petition the Court for a conservatorship, you are asking the Court to appoint a person to administer the financial affairs of the incapacitated person. These proceedings are generally very expensive, and can take as long as three to four months to complete. In addition, the Court will closely supervise the conservator's actions and will ask for a financial plan and periodic accountings.

Due to the Court's supervision under a conservatorship, it can be very difficult to accomplish Medicaid planning. In some instances, the Court may not allow the conservator to make transfers of assets, or purchase certain exempt items. In fact, some recent court cases in other states have indicated that the Court will not allow any kind of Medicaid planning by the conservator. For these reasons, it is essential that, if an individual requires Medicaid planning, he have an appropriately executed Power of Attorney.

Another part of Medicaid planning is maintaining eligibility once it is accomplished. One of the most common ways people become ineligible for Medicaid, after they have been on the program for some time, is by receiving funds that increase their countable assets over the $2,000 limit. This usually happens when the recipient receives monies through an inheritance, or as a designated beneficiary.

If the recipient is named as a designated beneficiary on any insurance policies, IRAs, retirement plans, or bank accounts, the financial institution will automatically pay benefits to the designated beneficiary (in this case the Medicaid recipient) when the original owner dies. When this happens, and the amount received is over the $2,000 allowable limit, the recipient will become ineligible for Medicaid and will have to begin privately paying for their care.

Another common way of becoming ineligible is through an inheritance. For example, when a married couple has simple "sweet heart" wills that give everything to the spouse first and then to the children, and one spouse is on Medicaid, the Medicaid recipient will become ineligible for benefits if the well spouse dies first and leaves the recipient an inheritance over the $2,000 limit.

To eliminate these problems, a proper Medicaid plan should include steps to remove the Medicaid recipient from all beneficiary designations on all assets that allow for such designations. In addition, the well spouse should also change his will so that the Medicaid recipient does not receive funds from the spouse outright, rather the will should provide for some form of special needs trust to receive the funds intended for the Medicaid recipient.

Finally, proper Medicaid plans should also make sure that all transfers and retitling are handled properly. For example, if the residence is still under a mortgage, and the property needs to be retitled as part of the Medicaid plan, the individual should check with the lender to make sure that the mortgage agreement allows for retitling. Some mortgage agreements state that retitling will trigger an acceleration clause that will enable the lender to call in the note upon any retitling. In addition, the new deeds will have to be properly filed with the appropriate clerk to fulfill the local recording requirements.

For transfers, you will want to make sure that the transfers are done in such a way as to avoid as much of the state and federal taxes as possible, for both the individual making the transfer, and the person receiving the asset. You will also want to make sure a gift tax return is filed for all transfers over the $11,000 federal yearly limit.

Summary

Long-term care planning should be a major concern for everyone, and especially for the elderly or disabled. Unless you begin your long term care planning early, are able to purchase a comprehensive long term care insurance plan, or have a large amount of assets at your disposal, you may need to consider Medicaid planning. As you can see from this chapter, Medicaid planning is a complex area with many pitfalls. It is recommended that you consult an elder law attorney who is competent in Medicaid planning, if you are contemplating long-term care planning.

EPILOGUE: A PERSONAL VIEW

Time

Time is an equal opportunity employer. Each human
*   being has exactly*
the same number of hours and minutes every day. Rich
*   people can't*
buy more hours. Scientists can't invent new minutes.
*   And you can't*
save time to spend it on another day. Even so time is
*   amazingly fair*
and forgiving. No matter how much time you've wasted
*   in the past,*
you still have an entire tomorrow. Success depends
*   upon using it*
wisely — by planning and setting priorities.
*   — Denis Waitely*

Time. The inexhaustible commodity that you cannot buy, sell, or accumulate. It is limitless in the sense that there is enough for everyone. It is limited, in that every person has only a measured portion and no more. It may be used, but it cannot be possessed. Curious that such an elusive element as time sometimes becomes the enemy of estate planning. How can this be so?

Earlier in this book, I stated that only about 20% of Americans have a will. The trust department of an Eastern bank engaged a study to determine the reasons people do not take the opportunity to plan for the disposition of their estates at death. The excuses given were the following:

1. I am unwilling to accept my mortality.
2. I am unwilling to pay the cost for preparing an estate plan.
3. I am unwilling to purchase life insurance or other products crucial to the success of an estate plan.
4. I am unwilling to discuss sensitive family matters with an attorney.
5. I can't make decisions.
6. I don't like/trust my kids and find it difficult to know how to distribute my estate at death.
7. I am stingy and won't make lifetime gifts to save taxes later.
8. I will do it tomorrow.

Procrastination — the thief of time — robs many people of the opportunity to successfully complete their estate planning goals. Admittedly, there are some people who do not view wealth accumulation as a goal, and do not, therefore, stress its conservation or transmission. However, there are others who seem to place much emphasis on acquiring riches, and it has always surprised me to encounter those individuals who have successfully attained their goals, and have accumulated great wealth, but who seem to have little interest in preserving it. It is as though, in the feverish activity of accumulating material things, there is a loss of the awareness of our mortality. I have actually had clients die on the eve of their appointment to sign wills and trusts which had been resting in my file for many months. It is naive to assume that we have so mastered time that there will always be tomorrow.

Time also creates changes in the circumstances of life which make an estate plan outdated. A will or trust, which may be proper while your children are minors, is not usually appropriate once they attain adulthood. An estate plan which may be adequate when the value of assets is relatively nominal will no longer be suitable when the accumulated assets reach taxable proportions. The planning for a single person is certainly not fitting for a married couple. A timely tax plan can be instantly made obsolete by changes in the tax laws. I always stress to my clients that estate planning is not an event which we attend and then immediately forget. It is a process which continues to require review and alteration as personal and financial circumstances change with the passage of time.

The matters discussed in this epilogue come from my estate planner's soul, rather than my intellect. The manual you have read was not written as a commercial venture. It is the outgrowth of forty years of meeting with clients of all ages and circumstances. After the initial client meeting to discuss the estate planning techniques most suited to the individual seated before me, I am frequently asked for direction to a book or reading material where additional information can be found and studied. Although there are many excellent books available, many of them contain more information than the client ever wanted to know about the subject, and the material is not specifically adapted to Colorado law. It is my sincere desire that my friends, clients, and others reading this book will find in it positive and helpful ideas for building up an estate, preserving the fruits of their labors, and transferring the unused portion to their families and charities.

Estate planning is both a science and an art. As a science, it involves the use of tax tables, formulas, legal documents, mathematics, and purely objective techniques. As an art, estate planning is subjective. Emotional. Intensely personal. When a client comes to see an estate planner, the client may have some fuzzy ideas about the desired disposition of the estate, but the client generally does not know exactly what the goals may be. As a result, the estate planner is more than a dispenser of technical information. The estate planning attorney or financial planner is a counselor. People are the proper subjects of estate planning, not just things.

Most of the horror stories that one hears about wills, trusts, and estate planning result from poorly conceived, or implemented, advice by those entrusted with the secrets of estate planning. Sometimes this is because the client is not forthright and honest with the advisers. At other times, the adviser tries to cram the client into a preconceived mold. Although the great majority of people fit into a rather limited number of well-defined patterns, the slavish use of forms will surely work injustice in the unique situations.

Let me caution the reader against undue concentration on the "dead-hand" approach to estate planning. This is the tendency to control people and property from beyond the grave. Few things are personally more objectionable to me than the attempt to manipulate the lives of family and friends by the manner in which financial favors are either withheld, or dispensed, in wills and trusts. Obviously, it is important to safeguard property against unwise use by persons who, due to age, or the circumstances of life, are incapable of wisely managing their own financial affairs. The danger is that we can overdo this and turn people into financial puppets.

Wealth accumulation and transmission are concerns as old as man. In Proverbs 22:3, the Bible states that, "A prudent man foresees the difficulties ahead and prepares for them; the simpleton goes blindly on and suffers the consequences." The subjects of probate and estate planning are so often associated with dying that many people strive to delay the process until the last minute, and then miscalculate the amount of time remaining. Again, in those cases, time becomes the enemy.

Perhaps a philosophical epilogue such as this seems out of place in a book designed primarily to convey facts and techniques. But it is my hope that this chapter of the book will focus the reader's attention on the true goal of estate planning, which is planning the lifetime care and use of property — ours while we still have time and health to use it, and later for friends, family, and charities. That is why the professional advisors who engage in the business of estate planning have such a solemn responsibility to dispense accurate and sensitive advice. And that is the perspective from which I hope you will review and utilize the information in this book.

An epilogue is defined as a short addition, or concluding section, at the end of any literary work, often dealing with the future of its characters. In this case, the characters are those of you who have read this book. Your future includes seeking out the best avenues for passing on your hard-earned and prized possessions to those dear to you, or other deserving beneficiaries. I would say, "Good luck," but estate planning is not a matter of luck at all. Instead, let me urge you to be wary of time, and use the knowledge which you have gained from this book to help you plan for what lies ahead.

GLOSSARY

Adjusted gross estate: used only for federal estate tax purposes. The adjusted gross estate is the value of the decedent's estate for federal tax purposes figured by subtracting funeral and administrative expenses, debts, taxes, and certain other items from the total value of the estate.

Administrator: in states other than Colorado, one appointed by the court to administer the estate of the decedent where the decedent failed to appoint an executor in his will, or died without a will. The feminine form of administrator is "administratrix." However, in Colorado the single term "personal representative" is used whether the decedent had no will designating an executor or personal representative, or where the person was nominated to serve under the terms of a will.

Appreciation: growth in the fair market value of the property. The term usually refers to an increase due to fluctuation in the market value of the property, rather than changes in the property itself. Antonym: depreciation.

Beneficiary: one for whose benefit a trust is created, or one to whom the proceeds of insurance are payable.

Commingling: the placing together of property of various kinds. In community property states the term has special significance, and refers to the mixing of one spouse's separate property with community property or with separate property of the other spouse.

Community property: property acquired by either spouse during marriage, except by gift, will, or inheritance. This is a property system based on the theory that marriage is a partnership. There are eight community property states. Colorado is not a community property state.

Convenience account: a bank account established by one person (a) in the name of himself and another person (b), for the purpose of allowing either person to draw out money to be used for the benefit of the first person. A common example of such an account is the situation in which the first person is aged or ill, and is unable to go to the bank to obtain funds, so the account is established to allow a second person to draw funds for the "convenience" of the other.

Decedent: a deceased person. The term refers either to one who dies leaving a will, or to one who dies without a will.

Devise: (noun) in most states, a gift of real estate which is made by the will of a decedent; (verb) to give real estate by means of a will. In Colorado, this term includes a testamentary gift of either real or personal property.

Devisee: one who receives real estate or other property under the terms of a will.

Disposition: transmitting or directing property ownership, as in disposition of property by a decedent's will.

Durable power of attorney: a written authority for one person to perform specified actions on behalf of another, which authority is not affected by the lifetime disability of the one granting the power.

Encumbrance: a claim, lien, charge, or liability against property, such as a mortgage.

Estate: the entire property owned by a person, whether land or movable property. In the probate context, the term refers to all property left by a decedent.

Executor: in states other than Colorado, one who is appointed in the will of a decedent to manage the estate, and to carry out the directions in the will for disposition of the estate property. The feminine of executor is "executrix." However, in Colorado the single term "personal representative" is used whether the decedent had no will designating an executor or personal representative, or where the person was nominated to serve under the terms of a will.

Fair market value: the value of property that would be set by an owner willing (but not forced) to sell for cash, and a buyer willing (but not forced) to buy for cash, with both buyer and seller knowing all relevant facts. The fair market value of property is intended to be an estimate of value which is fair, economic, and reasonable under normal conditions.

Grantor: a person who transfers property, other than by will (where he would be called "testator") or trust (where he could be called "settlor"), to someone else (known as the "grantee"). The term is generally used to describe the one who transfers property by gift or by sale.

Holographic will: a will written entirely in the handwriting of the testator.

Intestate: a person is said to die intestate when he leaves no valid will to control the disposition of his property.

Joint tenancy with right of survivorship: generally, ownership of property by two or more persons who have the same interest in the property and own it together; all rights in the property pass to the survivor upon the death of any one joint tenant, and ultimately pass to the last survivor. Thus, the interest of a joint tenant is not included in his probate estate when he dies, since it passes automatically at the death of a joint owner, unless the joint tenant is the last survivor of all of the joint tenants.

Letters: a document of authority issued to a personal representative by the probate court showing his authority to serve as personal representative.

Liquidity: used to describe whether an asset can be converted into cash easily. For example, stock which can be easily sold has good liquidity; stock which cannot be easily sold has poor liquidity.

Personal representative: a general term which, depending upon the context, includes an executor, administrator, special administrator, or a successor to any such fiduciary. The personal representative administers the probate estate, collecting assets, paying debts and taxes, and distributing the remaining assets to the persons entitled to them under the laws of intestacy or under the terms of the will. In Colorado, the testator can direct that the personal representative be unsupervised and relatively independent of the control of the probate court.

Posting: giving public notice, generally by displaying a written announcement in an official, conspicuous place — attaching a notice to the courthouse bulletin board.

Probate: the procedure for proving to the satisfaction of the probate court that an instrument is the last will and testament of the decedent.

Quitclaim deed: the deed intended to transfer whatever interest the grantor had, if he had any at all. This deed is distinguished from a warranty deed, in which the grantor guarantees that he does have a certain interest.

Realty: land and mineral interests. This includes buildings located on the land, as well as crops and trees growing on the land. Synonyms: real estate, real property, or immovables.

Self-proving will: a will which does not require that the witnesses appear in court to prove that the will was properly signed by the testator, because after signing the will the testator and the witnesses signed an additional document (not part of the will but often immediately following the will) in which they swear before a notary public that the will was correctly signed.

Settlor: the maker of a trust. The party owning property that becomes the asset of the trust, which is managed by the trustee for the beneficiary. May also be called the trustor or the grantor of the trust.

Survivorship account: a bank account in the name of two or more persons in which the entire amount passes to the survivor or survivors upon the death of one of the owners. The account may be with a company other than a bank.

Tenants in common: ownership by two or more persons of the same piece of property, in which each has the right to use and occupy the property at the same time with all the other owners. This type of ownership differs from the "joint tenancy with right of survivorship," in that the interest of the deceased owner does not automatically pass to the survivors. Thus, a tenant in common may dispose of his interest by will.

Testator: one who has made a will; one who dies leaving a will. The feminine of testator is "testatrix."

Trust: a legal contract whereby property is transferred by the settlor to a trustee for the benefit of a beneficiary, to be managed according to the terms expressed in the trust agreement.

Glossary

Trustee: the person who holds the property in trust for the benefit of another person who is called the beneficiary.

Valuation: the act of ascertaining or estimating the worth of the property.

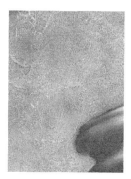

INDEX

Attestation clauses, 102
Attorneys' fees, 15, 17, 45
Authorization bank accounts,
124-125

B

Banks and bank accounts
asset protection, 191
jointly owned property, 124-125
personal representative status, 2,
15, 96, 115, 117-118
revocable living trusts. See
Revocable living trusts
Best use valuation, 22
Bonds
jointly owned property, 123-124
planning for debts and taxes, 28
probate estate coverage, 5-6
Bonds (surety)
personal representatives, 2, 96,
117
probate costs, 14
Boomerang gifts. See Charitable lead
annuity trusts (CLATs)
Burial expenses. See Funeral
expenses
Buy-sell agreements, 28, 170, 172

C

Cash contributions to charity, 70-71
Cash surrender value, 150
Charitable contributions, 69-84,
81-82
amount, 71
attributes of those who give, 70
boomerang gifts. See Charitable
lead annuity trusts (CLATs)
cash, 70-71
charitable remainder trusts. See
Charitable remainder trusts
CLATs. See Charitable lead
annuity trusts (CLATs)
community foundations, 82-83
culture and, 70

donor advised funds, 82-83
farms, 83
favorite causes, 69
fixed amount, 71
gift annuities, 84
income tax deductions, 71-72
life insurance, 72, 76
percentage, 71
personal residence, 83
planning for debts and taxes, 29
pooled income funds, 83-84
property, 70-71
religion and, 70
statistics on giving, 69
stock, 83
vacation homes, 83
volunteerism and, 70
wealth replacement trust, 76
Charitable foundations, 81-82
Charitable lead annuity trusts
(CLATs), 77-81
benefits, 79
compounding, 81
creation, 79
family limited partnerships, 81
gift tax consequences, 80
income tax consequences, 80
Jackie O example, 77-78
strategy, 77
tax-free wealth accumulation,
78-79
trustee selection, 80-81
unitrust compared, 79-80
Charitable remainder trusts, 72-76
benefits, 72
example, 74-75
formation, 72-73
tax consequences, 73-74, 75
Children. See Minors
CLATs. See Charitable lead annuity
trusts (CLATs)
Closely-held businesses, 165. See
also Family businesses
asset protection, 195-196

ABOUT OUR FORMS

Forms related to each section in this book — Estate Planning, Guardianship, Conservatorship, Informal Probate, Formal Probate, and Powers of Attorney are available from Bradford Publishing Co.

Bradford Publishing Co. forms related to Probate issues are identified with the prefix "CPC" (Colorado Probate Code) and are accepted in all Colorado Courts.

Please contact Bradford Publishing Co. for a complete list of the forms discussed in this book.

Bradford Publishing Co. also offers the *Colorado Will and Estate Planner* for individuals who want a simplified guide to plan for disability and death, and as a practical tool for attorneys to help clients organize their client's personal estate information.

This handy binder contains the basic information needed to understand and create a simple will, allocate assets to beneficiaries, and prepare for possible disability. It is divided into sections for information gathering, document preparation, and forms and checklists. The Planner also comes with a CD-ROM that contains PDF legal forms you can fill out on your computer, and print for your records.

To order forms, the *Colorado Will and Estate Planner,* or other fine Bradford products call 303-292-2590, fax 303-208-5014, or visit the web site and order online at www.bradfordpublishing.com.

800-446-2831

ABOUT BRADFORD PUBLISHING

Founded in 1881, Bradford Publishing Company is Colorado's oldest and most trusted publisher of legal forms and information. Today Bradford Publishing has an inventory of more than 800 legal forms and books specific to Colorado law. Our forms are accurate and up-to-date because we consult with attorneys and state agencies to keep them that way. All of our products are available on our website and many of our forms can be downloaded and completed on-screen. Bradford forms are accepted by the Colorado courts.

Visit the books section of our website to see our growing list of legal publications. If you live or work in the Denver Metro area, you can find all our books, forms and supplies at our store in lower downtown.

BRADFORD PUBLISHING COMPANY

1743 Wazee Street

Denver, Colorado 80202

800-446-2831

303-292-2590

303-298-4014 Fax

www.bradfordpublishing.com